CH00693595

M
SCOTTISH
KEERIOSITIES

ROBERT
HENDERSON

with a foreword by
JOHN RUNDLE

SAINT ANDREW PRESS
1995

Published by
SAINT ANDREW PRESS
121 George Street, Edinburgh EH2 4YN

Copyright © Robert Henderson 1995

ISBN 0 7152 0709 1

British Library Cataloguing in Publication Data
A catalogue record for this book
is available from the British Library

ISBN 0715207091

Design concept by Mark Blackadder.
Illustrations on pages 18, 107 by Michael Turnbull.
Etchings are taken from J Grant: *Old and New Edinburgh* (Cassell, 1887) in 3 vols; Samuel Green: *Scottish Pictures* (Religious Tract Society, 1891); J A Wylie: *The Scots Worthies* (Wm Mackenzie, 1880); Laurence Hutton: Literary Landmarks of Edinburgh (Osgood & McIlvaine, 1891); 'The Scottish Annals' from Macfarlane/Thomson: *The Comprehensive History of England* (Blackie & Sons 1861) in 12 vols.
Cover photographs by Robert Henderson.
Typeset in 11.5/14 pt Garamond.
Printed by Bell and Bain Ltd., Glasgow

CONTENTS

FOREWORD
by John Rundle

In my introduction to Robert Henderson's first volume of *Scottish Keeriosities*, I made the point that Scotland has an endless list of intriguing whimsies. As if to underline that, here we have a second compilation which demonstrates what an infinitely-fascinating nation it is when the tartan curtain is parted.

Behind lies the real show, where three-dimensional delights of all varieties wait to astonish and amuse – wells with healing powers; Britain's first manned aerial journey; a down-hill road that is actually uphill; the Vatican's ex-communication of Musselburgh – four acts from a glittering cast list that Director Henderson has on stage just long enough to keep interest at a peak before the next turn comes on with its own brand of entertainment.

Incidentally, Robert Henderson did much of his talent spotting in the pages of *The Scots Magazine*, thereby guaranteeing star performances every time.

Here is a man incandescent with pride as he shows his country to the world. Robert Henderson knows his Scotland all right. I'm just glad he wasn't competing against me when I took part in the BBC TV 'Super-Scot' quiz a few years ago.

[JOHN RUNDLE, Former Editor, *The Scots Magazine*]

PREFACE
by Robert Henderson

During the course of writing this book, I have been helped by various people in a number of different ways and I would like to offer them all my sincere thanks.

The following people contributed by drawing my attention to 'keeriosities' in particular areas:

Frances and Sandy Bryce (Renfrewshire); Neil Clement (Fife and Sutherland); Betty Gibson (Lanarkshire); Jim and Annette Hunter (Selkirk and Roxburghshire); Michael Lowndes (various locations); and John Randall (Peebleshire).

In addition, valuable and constructive comments on early drafts of the text were provided by my mother, Mary Henderson, by my late father-in-law, James Edgar, and by Harold Kyte.

I am also grateful to Derek Braid for his invaluable help in a number of areas, and to the late John Rundle, who kindly agreed to contribute a Foreword before his untimely death earlier this year.

Particular thanks are due to my sister-in-law, Anne Stiedl, who spent a considerable amount of time and effort reading each chapter and suggesting numerous improvements.

Lastly, and most important, this book

could never have been completed without the tremendous support, encouragement and practical assistance of my wife, Eileen, and the tolerance of my long-suffering children, Laura and Niall.

To them I owe a special debt.

INTRODUCTION

Whilst assembling information for the first volume of my book on *Scottish Keeriosities*, I came to realise that the supply of material for potential inclusion was much greater than I had anticipated. As a result it has been possible to identify a sufficient number of new themes to warrant a second volume.

For those who have yet to see a copy of the first book, it may be helpful to reiterate what is meant by the term '*keeriosity*'. This is a Scots word, meaning something that is strange or fascinating; and is the counterpart of the English word 'curiosity'.

To warrant inclusion in the book as a 'Scottish Keeriosity', I used two criteria: the first being that there has to be something tangible to be seen in Scotland; and the second that there needs to be an associated story which is not only thought to be true, but also has a strange or quirky element that makes the feature in some way peculiar and noteworthy. Eccentric personalities, whether good, bad, ugly or beautiful, have all left their mark – and with the passing of time even some of the less savoury events can now add colour to local histories. The keeriosities featured often reflect the trials and tribulations, triumphs and disasters of the times when they were erected.

The locations of all the keeriosities are shown in capital letters in the text. More detailed directions for finding the item referred to are given in the Geographical Index at the back of the book. An attempt has been made to exclude those keeriosities on private properties which are not regularly open to the public. This has been done both to make it easier for visitors to see the objects mentioned and to protect the privacy of property owners and their tenants. Inevitably perhaps there are one or two exceptions and these are marked in the Geographical Index by an asterisk. In these cases prior arrangements need to be made if the subject of interest is to be viewed.

As far as possible I have tried to verify that everything featured in the book can still be seen, but this cannot, of course, be guaranteed. We live in an ever-changing world and neither age, quality nor rarity value guarantees the survival and protection of our rich assortment of oddities. They can all too easily disappear. Threats to their future come from various sources. Artefacts such as milestones, unusual notices and funeral cairns have been destroyed by road building. Vandalism can deface and destroy items of interest. Theft is an ever-present threat. Sadly, an increasing number of churches and other public buildings are now kept locked because of the risks of theft and vandalism. Neglect also leads to the loss of unusual features as paintwork peels and old notices and signs become illegible. Natural processes of erosion and weathering are also at work, steadily obliterating many fascinating inscriptions on old buildings.

Fortunately, all is not lost. There are many encouraging signs that provide hope for the future protection and conservation of our heritage of curious items. Road engineers, when reconstructing the A9 road, took great care to move the historic Wade's Stone and to replace it as close as possible to its original site. Milestones are usually put back following road improvements, although not always pointing in the original direction, much to the confusion of unwary motorists (as travellers on the A75 near Creetown will discover). Historic sites and buildings are now better protected from deliberate destruction or are being found new uses. Old signs are being preserved and new memorials are being erected to commemorate recent as well as more distant events that have impacted on an area. And colourful local worthies continue to leave their distinctive legacies to amaze and amuse posterity.

Interest in local history is increasing and membership of conservation and heritage organisations is growing rapidly. Such trends augur well for the continued survival of our Scottish keeriosities.

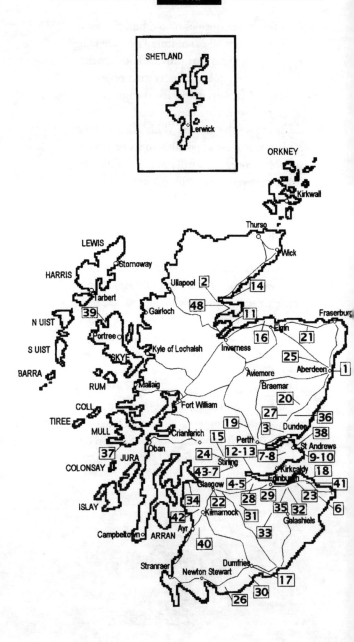

SHETLAND

Lerwick

ORKNEY

Kirkwall

Thurso

Wick

LEWIS

Stornoway

HARRIS

Ullapool **2**

14

48

Tarbert

39

Gairloch

11

Fraserburg

N UIST

Portree

Kyle of Lochalsh

Inverness

Elgin

16

21

25

S UIST

SKYE

Aviemore

Aberdeen **1**

BARRA

RUM

Mallaig

Braemar

20

COLL

Fort William

27

36

TIREE

19

3

Dundee

38

MULL

Crianlarich

15

Perth

7-8

St Andrews

37

Oban

24

12-13

9-10

JURA

Stirling

Kirkcaldy

18

COLONSAY

43-7

Edinburgh

41

Glasgow

4-5

28

29

23

34

22

35

32

6

ISLAY

42

Kilmarnock

31

Galashiels

Ayr

33

Campbeltown

ARRAN

40

Stranraer

Dumfries

Newton Stewart

17

26

30

MAP 1 — MADE FOR TRADE

MADE FOR TRADE

Ref	Location	Description
1	Aberdeen	Mercat cross
2	Ardgay	White Stone
3	Auchterhouse	Rush to pub after church
4	Bo'ness	Sea-Box Society crest
5	Bo'ness	Reversed 4 and sailing ship on gravestone
6	Bunkle	Pedlar's gravestone
7	Ceres	Tron, carved on Weigh House
8	Ceres	Stone figure of Provost
9	Crail	Customs House
10	Crail	Wright's sign
11	Cromarty	Tailor's sign
12	Culross	Sir George Bruce's house
13	Culross	Flesher's sign
14	Dornoch	Ell
15	Doune	Pistol making factory
16	Duffus	Mercat cross
17	Dumfries	Ell
18	Dunbar	Tolbooth
19	Dunkeld	Ell
20	Fettercairn	Ell
21	Fordyce	Minister threw snuff over wall
22	Glasgow	Templeton's carpet factory
23	Haddington	Stent Stane
24	Kilmadock	Pistol makers
25	Kintore	Tolbooth
26	Kirkcudbright	Billy Marshall's gravestone
27	Kirriemuir	Houses used as shops
28	Linlithgow	Cordiner's sign
29	Musselburgh	Tolbooth
30	New Abbey	Blacksmith's sign

MARKET SCENE, EDINBURGH'S HIGH STREET

MADE
FOR
TRADE

STOPPING *for* SHOPPING

Before the advent of 'seven-day opening' supermarkets there were shops, and before shops there were not-so-super markets where goods and livestock were traded on only one or two days a week.

Markets, super or otherwise, have come to be associated with towns. In the early days, the right to hold a market was restricted to burghs and this lucrative privilege was publicised by the presence of a mercat cross.

A mercat cross was seen as a status symbol and was viewed as the mediaeval equivalent of a modern shopping centre. To ensure it was suitably prominent, the cross was usually a tall stone shaft raised up on steps and capped by some sort of insignia. To confuse matters, few mercat crosses were topped by a cross. A notable exception can be seen at ORMISTON, East Lothian, where there is a fifteenth century cross. Royal burghs, with charters granted by the king, usually publicised their special status by crowning their crosses with heraldic beasts like unicorns. Many fine examples exist, parti-

The MERCAT CROSS, EDINBURGH

3

cularly in Fife within the former royal burghs.

The most ornate of the original crosses are the seventeenth century versions at **PRESTON**, East Lothian, and **ABERDEEN**. The latter has a unique series of what may be irreverently described as royal 'mug shots', with a display of ten carved stone portraits of all the Stewart kings. Both crosses are within circular rotunda from which the town crier used to make announcements. In this way mercat crosses took on the role not only of shopping centre, but also of local newspaper.

At one time there were close links between going shopping and going to church – Sunday trading was sometimes actually carried on right outside a church. Before the Reformation, fairs and markets were often held in churchyards, as indicated by the presence of a market cross. Moray District still has a number of examples within church-yards, such as that of St Peter's Church at **DUFFUS**. A close connection between church and shop can also be seen at **KIRRIEMUIR**, Angus, where a number of houses have windows facing on to the churchyard to allow goods to be sold on days when fairs were held.

Periodic Sunday markets lingered on in a few churchyards until the eighteenth century, when opposition from the Church finally prevailed. Sunday trading ceased outside the church of St Talarican in **FORDYCE**, Banff & Buchan, when the minister, Alexander Gallie, stormed into the churchyard, snatched up the bags of snuff that were on sale and threw their contents on to the ground outside the churchyard. Ministers had less control over what was sold outside the churchyard, and it was reported in the eighteenth century that as soon as the church service ended at AUCHTERHOUSE, Dundee, 'there was a rush to the change or ale house'. In their defence, no doubt, some parishioners might claim the minister's sermon had driven them to drink.

Shopping was closely regulated and rules were strictly enforced by the Dean of Guild, who was the counterpart of the modern Trading Standards Officer. To prevent fraudulent practices by unscrupulous merchants, national standards of weights and measures were laid down. The standard measure for length was an 'ell' (37.2 inches), for grain the 'firlot', for liquid the 'stoup'. These distinctive Scottish units of measure disappeared as Scotland changed over to the standard English imperial weights and measures following the Union of Parliaments in 1707.

A TALLY-
STICK,
dated 1692

Although no longer in use, some of these measures are still in evidence. The best known is the ell rod fixed to the wall of the Ell Shop in the square at DUNKELD, Perth & Kinross. This example is detachable and was used from the early eighteenth century for measuring cloth sold in the market. Other ells which are permanent fixtures can be seen on the tolbooth wall at DUMFRIES, Nithsdale, and on the mercat cross at FETTERCAIRN, Kincardine & Deeside. In DORNOCH, Sutherland, where a market in the churchyard still occurred as late as 1803, there is a stone with an ell length marked on it for measuring lengths of cloth.

To avoid disputes about the accuracy of weights the burgh's own set were used on the tron or public weigh-beam. Since a tron was made of wood, none has survived. However, one has been reconstructed at STENTON in East Lothian, and another, with a bale being weighed on it, is carved in stone above the door of the weigh-house in CERES, North East Fife.

RESTRICTIVE PRACTICES

Fair competition was a concept that held little appeal to local shopkeepers (merchants) or producers (craftsmen) in the burghs. The basic concern was to protect their interests at the expense of local consumers or outside producers. This was done in several ways. Burghs were given a virtual trading monopoly so that all goods had to be sold within them, and royal burghs had the additional privilege of the exclusive and highly profitable right to engage in overseas trade. This allowed those merchants involved in foreign trade to become extremely wealthy.

Thus they considered themselves to be the elite and, to look the part, they were generally snappy dressers. One of their number still continues to look down on the populace at large. The elegantly attired figure of John Cowane, who made his fortune trading with Holland, gazes stonily down from the walls of the Guildhall in STIRLING. His statue is affectionately known as 'Auld Staney Breeks'.

Another ploy to reduce competition was to impose a toll or customs duty on goods brought into market from outside a burgh. The burgh boundary was therefore important, given the privileges bestowed within it. In some cases the boundary was marked by a distinctive feature, such as the White Stone on the eastern edge of **PEEBLES**, Tweeddale. Another white quartz stone, known as 'Clach Eiteag', marking a place of trade, can be seen in the square at **ARDGAY**, Sutherland. In the past it is said to have been moved from parish to parish to mark the site of the local market. By the eighteenth century it had come to mark the site of the November fair in the parish of Kincardine at which cattle and farm produce were sold.

The dues that outsiders had to pay were sometimes collected on entry either at the town gate or on a narrow bridge. The best example of the former is the West Port in **ST ANDREWS**, North East Fife, and of the latter the old bridge at **STIRLING**.

Occasionally the actual site where custom dues (or 'stents') were collected within a burgh is still marked. In **HADDINGTON**, East Lothian, the Stent or Customs Stone, which provided a cold rather than hot seat for the tax collector while he gathered in custom dues, can still be seen. Another stone associated with the payment of dues is to be found in the churchyard at **RESCOBIE**, Angus. A scooped-out basin in the stone is said to have been used to measure the payment in grain which every trader was required to make to the local laird at the annual St Troddan's Fair.

In ports with an active overseas trade, the collection of duties would be overseen from a Customs House. One dating from the seventeenth century can be identified by the sailing ship carved on the door lintel at CRAIL, North East Fife.

Tolls were often collected in a booth and such toll-booths eventually evolved into centres for local tax gathering. Laws needed to be passed to authorise and set local tax levels and such laws needed to be enforced. By this process tolbooths developed into the local centre for administration, taxation and law enforcement. Their importance is reflected in the many impressive tolbooths or town houses to be seen in former burghs such as DUNBAR, East Lothian, TAIN, Ross & Cromarty, and KINTORE, Gordon.

Not everyone was impressed, however, and the construction of the tolbooth in MUSSEL-BURGH, East Lothian, actually led to the rare situation whereby the town was excommuni-cated for 200 years. To build the tolbooth in 1590, stones were taken from the ruins of the nearby Chapel of Our Lady of Loretto, which had been destroyed in 1544. This initiative in recycling resources was not appreciated by the Vatican, which saw it as an act of sacrilege and decided to excommunicate the town.

Trading activities owed more to the needs of Mammon than the heeds of the Church. Another ruse designed to restrict competition was to allow only local property owners or burgesses to engage in craft or trading activities. To prevent any challenge to this cosy arrangement, these same people ensured that they were also the only ones allowed to vote in burgh council elections. Within the council one of their number was chosen as leader or Provost. CERES, North East Fife, has

one of the most popular holders of this title
in Scotland. This is not so much because he is
dead (he is literally stone cold), but because
of the appealing nature of the small stone
figure. He looks rather like an oversized Toby
Jug and is reputed to be a likeness of the last
provost to be appointed by the church in
1578. This engaging character still holds an
elevated position at the centre of Ceres life,
thanks to his lofty perch in a wall by the
crossroads.

WELFARE *before the* WELFARE STATE

Both merchants and craftsmen formed themselves into Trade or Merchant Guilds. A
prime function of the Guilds was to promote
the financial interests of their members, and
the range of restricted practices which they
indulged in would have made any hard-line
twentieth century trade union leader envious.
The Guilds came to control and run local
political and economic life, so it is hardly
surprising that the needs of their members
took precedence over those of the rest of the
community.

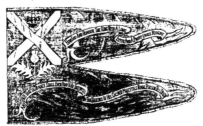

The BLUE BLANKET *or* STANDARD
of the INCORPORATED TRADES *of* EDINBURGH

The Guilds also had a welfare role – to dispense charity to members and their families falling on hard times. It would be difficult to find anyone falling on harder times than 'William McPherson and two others whose tongues were cut out by the Turks of Algiers. All three in a melancholy state'. Another to suffer from Algerian pirates, fortunately less severely in physical terms, was 'James Campbell taken by the Algerians in a vessel called the Swallow. After three years slavery released by a Maltese ship of war'. All received financial help in 1749 and 1748 respectively from the curiously named Sea-Box Society in Bo'ness, West Lothian. This Society was formed in 1634 and took its name from the sea-chest into which seafaring merchants from the town were expected to make a donation of 10% of their profits on returning from a successful voyage. The funds were used for charitable purposes and the Society is commemorated by its crest on a tenement in Corbiehall, BO'NESS.

When individuals rather than institutions undertook charitable acts, they were rarely reluctant to publicise their acts of generosity. The notion of anonymous giving held little appeal when the alternative was self-publicity. Above the door of the Guildhall – formerly Cowane's Hospital in STIRLING – a plaque proudly proclaims: 'This Hospital Was Erected And Largely Provyded By John Cowane Deane Of Guild For The Entertainment Of Decayed Gild Breither. John Cowane 1639'. Those housed in the building may not have been too happy about being described as

'Decayed', or about 'The Entertainment' which seems to have amounted to a list of enjoyable activities which were banned – but at least they had a sound roof over their heads. Whether their poor neighbours in STIRLING enjoyed any more entertainment in their house – dating from 1530 and 'Foundit For Support Of The Puir By Robert Spittal Taillyour To King James The 4' – is uncertain.

The most impressive example of a philanthropic development comes not from the old town of Stirling, but from an industrial mill village on the Clyde – NEW LANARK, Clydesdale. Such is the outstanding importance of this village that it has been designated a 'World Heritage' site. This fascinating place was developed from 1795 onwards by two remarkable men with social consciences – first by David Dale and then by his son-in-law, Robert Owen. By 1800, the cotton mill had become the largest in Scotland. Although 2500 people were to live and work in the village, it was not its size so much as the revolutionary social policies and humanitarian ideals pursued at New Lanark, particularly by Robert Owen, that were to catch the popular imagination.

DAVID DALE

At a time when most mill owners were exploiting child labour and showing little concern for the welfare of their employees, Owen offered a new vision for the future. Not only did he refuse to allow children under ten to work in the mills, but he actually provided a school for them, where a wide curriculum was taught in a relaxed atmosphere based on kindness rather than punishment. The housing provided for the workforce was of good quality. A social centre, known grandly as The Institute for the Formation of Character, was built for both educational and recreational activities and included a library. The shop sold quality goods at low prices, with profits being used to provide community facilities. This concept became the inspiration for the co-operative movement.

SELF-PUBLICITY

Robert Owen's attitude to prices and profits would have been incomprehensible to most members of the Merchant Guilds, who much preferred to retain rather than redistribute their profits. A favourite way of drawing attention to financial success and impressing the neighbours was for a merchant to build himself a large house. In 1597 George Bruce, having made a fortune trading coal from Fife, built himself an imposing house at CULROSS, Dunfermline. To ensure that everyone knew who owned it, he had his initials – 'GB' – displayed prominently on the gable. Further profits allowed him to build such an impressive extension in 1611 that the building became known as Culross Palace. By this time he had been given a knighthood, and to publicise the fact he was now Sir George Bruce he had the letters 'SGB' put on the front of the house.

If not names, then trades signs were prominently displayed. The Merchant Guilds

used as their symbol the figure '4', which was
sometimes reversed. It was first adopted in
Scotland by the Stirling Merchant Guild and
a reversed 4 can be seen on the lamps outside
the old Guildhall in STIRLING. At BO'NESS,
West Lothian, the reversed 4, together with
a sailing ship, is shown on the gravestone of
a merchant, clearly indicating that he was
wealthy enough to trade abroad using his
own ship. No doubt he was a Sea-Box man.

Craftsmen or tradesmen, as well as merchants, were keen to draw attention to their
status, preferably while still alive, by displaying their trade sign. The hammermen's
(metalworkers) view of themselves as the elite
was encouraged by the fact that only they and
the cordiners (shoemakers) were allowed to
use a crown on their sign. Their proud boast
– 'By hammer and hand all arts to stand' – is
on a blacksmith's sign of 1775, above a
former smithy at NEW ABBEY, Nithsdale.
On the front of a building in the High Street,
LINLITHGOW, West Lothian, there is the
badge of the cordiners, showing their
distinctively shaped cutting tool, a crown
and a surrounding of oak leaves. The leaves
symbolise the oak bark, which was placed in
the water where the hides were soaked, to
provide the tanning.

Other trade signs still to be seen on houses
include a tailor's scissors and flat iron (dated
1727) at CROMARTY, Ross & Cromarty, a
flesher's (butcher's) cleaver and steelyard
(1664) at CULROSS, Dunfermline, and a
wright's knife and compass (1643) at CRAIL,
North East Fife.

The most impressive display of trade signs is to be found on gravestones. In contrast with England, Scotland has a fascinating and very rich heritage of carved seventeenth and eighteenth century headstones portraying the tools of trade of everyone from butchers and bakers to gardeners and gamekeepers, from millers and miners to smiths and schoolmasters.

SPECIALISATION

Although most burghs had a range of trades represented, certain towns became known for specialising in particular products. Forfar and Selkirk were famous for their shoemakers, who were known either as 'souters', from the Latin word *sutor*, meaning shoemaker, or 'cordiners' from the French word *cordonnier* meaning leather worker. Surprisingly, the shoemakers seem to have left a large market unexploited, perhaps because it was already being exploited by the male sex at large. As one commentator on Scotland wrote in 1689: 'Their ordinary 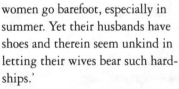 women go barefoot, especially in summer. Yet their husbands have shoes and therein seem unkind in letting their wives bear such hardships.'

Men were only too keen to let their long-suffering wives endure hardships. The fishermen of Banffshire, for instance, put pressure on their wives to wade out to meet the returning boats and carry the men ashore; the justification being that this kept the men's long leather boots dry. If there was heavy work to be done, then this usually fell to the women. After all, this was cheaper for their husbands than buying a horse. In eighteenth century Caithness it was the practice for the women to carry creels full of manure from the dunghills to the fields. The men's contribution, it seems, was confined to helping their wives by filling the creels for them.

Pistols are products not often associated with women, although given the way that women were exploited they must have been tempted to use them against the male sex. Guns are also rarely associated with beauty, but the intricately decorated versions produced at DOUNE, Stirling, from 1646 until the end of the eighteenth century, were notable exceptions. These ornate pistols were much sought after throughout Europe. The old factory building has been restored and the graves of pistol makers, of whom the Caddell family were the most famous, can be seen not far away in KILMADOCK churchyard.

Far more important to man's well-being than making pistols is the production of food. Mills have played a key role in this process by grinding cereal crops into flour for use in baking bread; a fact clearly but simply spelled out by the words 'No mill, No meal' on the gable of the former mill, now the Millhouse Hotel at STEWARTON, Kilmarnock & Loudoun. Not far away at STAIR, Cumnock & Doon Valley, is a factory with the appealing name of the Tam o' Shanter and Water of Ayr Hone Works. This hone from home is produced

from local stones and the honestones are used
for sharpening.

The most interesting and also the most
eccentric looking industrial building in
Scotland must be the former Templeton's
carpet factory in GLASGOW. This extra-
ordinary structure was completed in 1890
and has a magnificent display of colourful
and ornate brickwork producing a touch of
Byzantium beside Glasgow Green. After
three designs were rejected by the city
authorities, an exasperated James Templeton
asked his architect, William Leiper, what he
considered to be the most outstanding building in the world. On advising him that it
was the Doge's Palace in Venice, Leiper was
instructed to model his design on that building. The city fathers were impressed and a
touch of the East was brought to Glasgow's
East End.

Glasgow's Doge's Palace produced the
carpets, with a pile one inch thick, for the
luxury liner Queen Mary. This ship, like the
carpets, was made on the Clyde and an
unusual legacy from the early days of ship-
building remains embedded in the mud at
PORT GLASGOW, Inverclyde. A series of
wooden stakes, clearly visible in the mud at
low tide, mark the positions of ponds where
timber was kept to prevent it from drying
out before it was used to build the ships.

Peddling their WARES

Ships were vital for trade to and from the
Scottish islands, but in most of the remoter

rural areas the availability of goods from elsewhere depended on itinerant traders such as
tinkers, pedlars and packmen. They were the
equivalent of the mobile shop, but had no
worries about petrol prices since they used
either horses or shanks's pony. The tools of a
pedlar's trade are shown on the gravestone of
Patrick James in BUNKLE churchyard,
Berwickshire. The stone dates from 1739 and
shows his horse, scales and bulk measure. His
wife, also portrayed on the stone, was doubt-
less relieved that the burden of carrying in
this case was borne by the horse. The trade
marks of a tinker were crossed spoons and
rams' horns and can be seen at KIRKCUD-
BRIGHT, Stewartry, on the gravestone of Billy
Marshall, who is reputed to have lived to the
age of 120.

A long life-span was extremely unusual
because itinerant traders faced many hazards
that threatened their health and safety. Travelling in remote areas and carrying their wares
and money with them, such traders were
tempting targets for thieves. During one
robbery on the Isle of Skye – carried out by
two brothers named Buchanan – the pedlar
was killed when he put up a struggle, and his
body was thrown into a river gorge. A lad who
helped the brothers mind sheep witnessed
the event and was sworn to tell no living soul.
However, his conscience troubled him and
after a few days he escaped from the brothers
and made his way to the manse at Snizort.

It was all too apparent to the minister
that something terrible had happened, but the
lad, bound by his oath, refused to say what it

was. The minister went with him to SNIZORT Church and suggested he told the Baptismal Stone what he had seen. The wily minister then hid in the church and on overhearing the story informed the authorities of the murder. One of the brothers was tracked down and tried in Portree, where he became the last person to be hanged on Skye.

Another hazard facing these travelling salesmen was a greater chance of coming into contact with infectious diseases. Such a fate befell the unfortunate John Jones, a pedlar on the Isle of Mull. In one of the cottages he called at, he found the family stricken by smallpox. He selflessly nursed them before continuing on his travels. He had not gone far when he himself suffered a severe attack of smallpox. Unable to continue, he stopped by a pool on the RIVER LUSSA, where he died on 1st April 1891, aged 60. He, along with his pack, was buried at this spot, which is marked by a small cairn, beside what became known as the Pedlar's Pool.

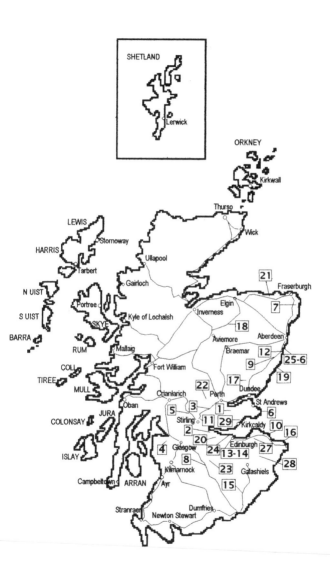

SHETLAND

Lerwick

ORKNEY

Kirkwall

Thurso

Wick

LEWIS

Stornoway

HARRIS

Ullapool

Tarbert

Gairloch

21

Fraserburgh

N UIST

Elgin

7

S UIST

Portree

Inverness

18

BARRA

SKYE

Kyle of Lochalsh

Aviemore

Aberdeen

RUM

Braemar

12

COLL

Mallaig

9

25-6

TIREE

Fort William

17

19

MULL

Crianlarich

22

Dundee

Oban

5

3

Perth

St Andrews

COLONSAY

JURA

Stirling

1

6

11

29

Kirkcaldy

10

2

20

16

ISLAY

4

Glasgow

24

Edinburgh

27

13-14

28

Kilmarnock

8

23

Galashiels

Campbeltown

ARRAN

Ayr

15

Stranraer

Dumfries

Newton Stewart

MAP 2 — TIME AND TIDE

TIME AND TIDE

Ref	Location	Description
1	Abdie	Sundial on Pictish stone
2	Airth	Sundial on mercat cross
3	Auchterarder	Hourglass
4	Bishopton	Text about time
5	Callander	Sundial and verse
6	Crail	Weather vane
7	Crimond	Clock with 61 minutes
8	Douglas	Clock chimes early
9	Drumlithie	Bell for weavers
10	Dunbar	Barometer pedestal
11	Dunblane	Weather vane
12	Dunnottar	Hourglass
13	Edinburgh	Clock on Balmoral Hotel
14	Edinburgh	Hourglass
15	Ewes	Bell up tree
16	Eyemouth	Memorial to storm victims
17	Glamis	Multiple dial
18	Grantown-on-Spey	War funded clock
19	Inverbervie	Tolbooth bell
20	Linlithgow	'Wee Meg Duncan' bell-clapper
21	Macduff	Faceless clock
22	Muthill	Multiple dial
23	New Lanark	Bell brought by Highlanders
24	South Queensferry	Mass dial
25	Stonehaven	Pedestal sundial
26	Stonehaven	Barometer
27	Wester Pencaitland	Sundial on mercat cross
28	Westruther	Coaching clocks
29	Windygates	Dairy clock

TIME AND TIDE WAIT FOR NO MAN

Dialling the TIME

Before the introduction of the speaking clock it was still possible to dial the time– thanks to the introduction of sundials. However, the vagaries of the Scottish climate meant that this method of keeping track of the time of day was a very hit or miss affair. Although a sundial has a face rather like a clock's, instead of two hands it has a single, fixed and pointed hand known as a 'gnomon', which in sunshine casts a shadow that moves around the dial during the course of the day.

Sundials were often placed in a prominent position where they could readily be seen by local people. One of the most popular sites was on a mercat cross – such as those at AIRTH, Falkirk, and WESTER PENCAITLAND, East Lothian.

Another type of sundial calibrated to show church activities (also known as a Mass Dial) was placed on the south wall of a church and used to denote the times of church services. An example can be seen at SOUTH QUEENSFERRY near the Forth Bridge. In coastal communities geared to nautical activity, a site close to the harbour was often chosen. An interesting example can be seen at STONEHAVEN, Kincardine & Deeside, where there is a pedestal sundial by the pier steps, dating from 1710.

Probably the most unusual sundial is at **ABDIE**, North East Fife, where a seventh century carved Pictish symbol stone has been converted into a sundial. This remarkable stone was subsequently put to yet another use when it was utilised by the Ordnance Survey for one of its arrow-shaped bench marks.

As the functional value of sundials declined with the development of more reliable timepieces, so they became popular decorative features, usually set on a stone plinth in gardens or on the walls of houses, particularly from the seventeenth century on-wards. It became fashionable to have cheerful mottos or verses inscribed on sundials, usually with a theme related to time. One of this type at **CALLANDER**, Stirling, is inscribed:

> *I mark not the hours unless they bring light,*
> *I mark not the hours of darkness and night,*
> *My promise is solely to follow the sun,*
> *And point out the course his chariot doth run.*

Some pithy advice about not wasting time is given in the garden of Formakin Ho1se, near **BISHOPTON**, Renfrew:

> *Yesterday Returneth Not*
> *Tomorrow Perchance Cometh Not*
> *Today Is Thine*
> *Misuse It Not.*

To impress the neighbours, it seems that a single dial was insufficient. Much more spectacular, and hence expensive, is a multiple dial. This is a large vertical sundial with each face covered by numerous small individual dials of all shapes, sizes and types. There can be up to 80 separate dials with both raised metal and sunken stone 'gnomons'. An impressive example can be found in the grounds of Drummond Castle, near MUTHILL, Perth & Kinross. It dates from 1630 and was built by the Master Mason to King Charles I.

Scotland's largest sundial is found in the grounds of the castle at GLAMIS, Angus. It stands 21 feet high and has 84 individual dials. Whether they all tell the same time is an interesting question. These multiple dials are a Scottish speciality and Scotland has a unique collection of them. It seems strange that such a passion for sundials should be so intense in a northern clime not generally noted for its sunshine record.

clocking on

Since it was possible to dial the time only on a sunny day, it was just a matter of time before a more reliable timepiece came into use. The oldest working public clock in Scotland is in DOUGLAS, Clydesdale, and is said to have been gifted by Mary, Queen of Scots in 1565. Despite its age, this clock can never be accused of being behind the times – it chimes three minutes before each hour. This reflects the town's links with the powerful Douglas family whose motto, along with that of the town clock, is 'Never Behind'.

In contrast, a clock at CRIMOND, Banff & Buchan, is in perpetual danger of falling behind time. Although the clock face proclaims in large letters that 'The Hour's Coming', closer scrutiny suggests that the hour is likely to be late in arriving. Whereas elsewhere an hour is the standard 60 minutes, according to the church clock it lasts for 61 minutes in Crimond. The last section of the hour on the clock face has six rather than the usual five minutes marked on it, thanks to an oversight by the clockmaker.

An inaccuracy of one minute an hour or 24 minutes per day would have been perfectly acceptable nearly 300 years ago. In 1703 Elgin's clock-man had 'to keep the town's clock so right in her going as that she shall not go half an hour wrong backward or forward in twenty four hours'.

For most of the twentieth century there has been one clock that was deliberately kept at the wrong time. The clock on the North British Hotel above Waverley Station in EDINBURGH was always kept 2¹/₂ minutes ahead. This practice dated from the building's origins as a railway hotel. The idea was not to mislead, but on the contrary to be helpful, by ensuring that passengers using this clock would always have a little extra time to spare to catch their train. The hotel has recently been renovated and renamed The Balmoral Hotel. Fortunately, this interesting tradition has been re-established.

Other unusual clocks that also owe their origins to a particular form of transport can still be seen showing the time on a lodge gatehouse at WESTRUTHER, Berwickshire. They date from the coaching era and are thoughtfully positioned at eye level for a stagecoach driver. If time seems to stand still at Westruther, it is not surprising – closer perusal reveals that these very realistic-looking clocks are actually painted on to the stonework. Since a stagecoach would always pass the clock at the predicted time, it seems an ingenious way of guaranteeing that the stage would have an immaculate record for keeping to its timetable!

Although the clocks at Westruther at least tell the correct time twice a day, even this luxury is denied to the faceless clock in the tower of Doune Church at **MACDUFF**, Banff & Buchan. In fact the tower has clock faces on three sides, but the fourth one, facing the neighbouring town of Banff, is blank. This is said to reflect the contempt felt by the people of Macduff towards their neighbours who, in 1701, advanced the town clock to bring forward by an hour the execution of James Macpherson, a local freebooter. This was done to ensure that a pardon, which was rumoured to be on its way, did not arrive on time. The clock face was left empty to remind the townsfolk of Banff of the occasion when they chose to remain ignorant of the correct time.

A clock, whose curiosity value lies in the inscription rather than in the face, can be found at **WINDYGATES**, Kirkcaldy, where it was 'Erected from the proceeds of Social Betterment Dairy Scheme'. This was not so much a novel method of indicating that it was a time of milk surpluses, as a scheme devised by the government during World War I to persuade people to drink milk rather than alcohol. A change in drinking habits was considered necessary for strategic reasons, as the production of munitions was being hampered by the workforce's taste for alcohol.

Another clock paid for through wartime fund-raising can be seen in **GRANTOWN-ON-SPEY**, Badenoch & Strathspey. During the Napoleonic War funds were collected to help the war effort, but at Grantown the collection did not reach its target until hostilities were ending. To show that the time spent collecting had not been wasted, a clock was built with the proceeds and placed on Speyside House in the town square.

For **WHOM** *the* **BELL** *tolls*

Even if people cannot see the time, it is always possible that they might hear it instead. The most common way of ensuring this is to ring a bell. The tolbooth tower usually contained a bell, although it has generally been superseded in more recent times by a clock. At **INVERBERVIE**, Kincardine & Deeside, the former tolbooth bell of 1792 can be seen hanging on a wooden frame in Church Street. It was formerly rung to inform the local populace of the time at six and nine o'clock in the morning and two and nine o'clock in the afternoon and evening. Hours of work were also regulated by the bell. In the same district, at **DRUMLITHIE**, the bell in the tall circular tower, built in 1710, was rung to control the working hours of the local weaving community.

A bell was also used to summon the workers to the local mills in the remarkable village of **NEW LANARK**, Clydesdale (*see* chapter 1, 'Made for Trade'). The bell on the top of the 'New Buildings' is said to have been brought to New Lanark by people emigrating from the Highlands as a result of the notorious 'Clearances'. Their ship had been destined for North America, but lay stormbound in Greenock when David Dale made them an offer they couldn't refuse – namely the prospect of housing and employment in New Lanark.

The time for church services, as well as work, was announced by the ringing of a bell, usually located on the church roof, but unusually in the case of **EWES**, Annandale & Eskdale, it was placed in a tree. The church bell was put there as a temporary measure when the old kirk was being demolished and the new one built. The parishioners, however, became so used to the bell in this 'intreeging' position that they decided to retain it.

The Church of St Michael's, **LINLITHGOW**, West Lothian, has its three bells in a conventional belfry within the tower, but there is nothing conventional about the smallest of these bells. It is affectionately known as 'Wee Meg Duncan', after an old woman who used to live near the church and lambast any late-comers she saw hurrying to church. Meg Duncan's tongue is now immortalised in the clapper of this bell, which continues to ring after the other two bells have stopped. In this way Meg's custom of exhorting those arriving late for a service to hurry themselves is continued.

This same church also maintains a

distinctive tradition of ringing the bells shortly before the service ends. This originated not
as a means of waking up anyone who slept
through the sermon, but as a hint to the
coachmen who had brought families to the
service to vacate their places of liquid refresh-
ment and return to the church to pick up
their passengers.

Inside a church the sermon was timed by
means of a large and conspicuous hourglass
through which the sands of time ran. It was
customary for the sermon to last for one turn
of the glass, or one hour, but there was always
concern among the congregation that the
minister would turn the glass over again and
continue. Examples of hourglasses can still
be seen at Corstorphine, EDINBURGH, and
DUNNOTTAR, Kincardine & Deeside. The
glass at AUCHTERARDER, Perth & Kinross,
was interfered with so often, presumably by
disgruntled members of the congregation,
that it was put inside a protective iron frame.

Under PRESSURE

In the twentieth century, a common
complaint is to be short of time and under
pressure. In earlier periods the main pressure
that caused concern was of the atmospheric
variety, as this affects the weather and thereby
impinges directly on the activities of farmers
and fishermen. In fishing communities a
barometer near the harbour was a valuable
asset. STONEHAVEN, Kincardine & Deeside,
has one dating from 1852. At DUNBAR, East
Lothian, there is an impressive carved stone

pedestal for a barometer. It dates from 1856 and shows a fisherman being seen off in his boat by his family.

Careful perusal of such a barometer could help to ensure a fisherman's safe return to his family by providing early warning of the onset of low pressure with attendant strong winds and likelihood of storms. To be caught out at sea in such conditions could be disastrous. This is what happened to the EYEMOUTH, Berwickshire fishing fleet on 14th October 1881, with tragic results. A total of 24 boats were lost and 129 men were drowned, decimating the town's male population. A monument to this disaster, in the shape of a broken mast, can be seen in the old cemetery.

In contrast to the barometer, that other weather indicator, the weather vane, is usually placed as high as possible to catch the wind and to be easily seen. Church towers are popular sites and the most common symbol on church weather vanes is a cockerel. This bird is popular because it heralds the dawn of a new day and the end of night and darkness, with its associated fears. It is also associated with the Resurrection. The day of the Crucifixion started with the cock crowing three times and Simon Peter's denial that he was a follower of Jesus, but ended with new hope for the future of man.

The weather vane on top of the Cathedral at DUNBLANE, Stirling, is unusual – the cockerel has lost all interest in crowing and appears to be descending from his perch, apparently having decided his position is too exposed. A rather different creature tops the

weather vane on the tolbooth at CRAIL, North
East Fife. Its name – the 'Crail Capon' –
might suggest another chicken, but in fact
this Capon is a smoked haddock.

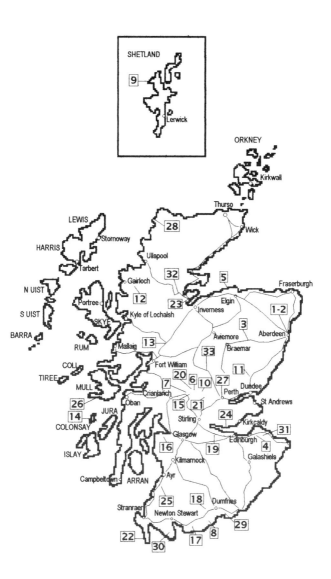

SHETLAND

9

Lerwick

ORKNEY

Kirkwall

Thurso

LEWIS

28

Stornoway

Wick

HARRIS

Tarbert

Ullapool

32

5

Fraserburgh

Gairloch

N UIST

12

23

Elgin

Portree

Inverness

1-2

S UIST

SKYE

Kyle of Lochalsh

3

Aberdeen

BARRA

Aviemore

RUM

Mallaig

13

Braemar

COLL

Fort William

33

11

TIREE

20

6

10

27

MULL

7

Dundee

Perth

26

Crianlarich

St Andrews

Oban

15

21

14

JURA

Stirling

24

COLONSAY

Kirkcaldy

31

Glasgow

19

Edinburgh

4

ISLAY

16

Galashiels

Kilmarnock

Campbeltown

ARRAN

Ayr

25

18

Dumfries

Stranraer

Newton Stewart

29

22

8

30

17

MAP 3 — HEALING WELL

HEALING WELL

Ref	Location	Description
1	Aberdeen	Inscribed water trough
2	Aberdeen	Water tap with face
3	Aboyne	Wells
4	Bolton	Well inscribed to Burns' mother
5	Burghead	Pictish well used for drownings
6	Camusvrachan	Lifting stones
7	Cashlie	Contraceptive stone
8	Dalbeattie	Slot Well
9	Eshaness	Gravestone of Donald Robertson killed in error
10	Fearnan	Measles stone
11	Glamis	Pictish cross slab with cauldron and legs
12	Innis Maree	Oak tree with coins in it
13	Invergarry	Well of the Heads
14	Isle of Colonsay	Lifting stone
15	Killin	St Fillan's healing stones
16	Kilmacolm	St Fillan's Well
17	Kirkcudbright	Well and inscription
18	Kirkpatrick Durham	St Patrick's Well
19	Linlithgow	Carved wellhead – St Michael's Well
20	Milton Eonan	Stone with Eonan's cross
21	Monzievaird	St Serfs Well
22	Mull of Logan	Dropping Cave
23	Munlochy	Cloutie well
24	North Queensferry	Well with figures fighting
25	Old Dailly	Lifting stones

Ref	Location	Description
26	Pennyghael, Mull	Memorial to Beatons
27	Perth	Neo-classical water tower
28	Rhiconich	Well for hospitality
29	Ruthwell	Brow Well
30	Sorbie	Source of leeches; White Loch of Ravenstone
31	Stenton	Mediaeval well
32	Strathpeffer	Institution for Poor Spa Drinkers
33	Struan	Whooping cough stone

HEALING
WELL,
FEELING WELL

Water is vital to sustain life and therefore its availability has always been crucial to every burgh, village, castle and house. Pollution of the water supply was a disaster which led to disease and death. It is hardly surprising that concerns about water supply are evident throughout Scotland.

DRINKING WELLS

Wells, fountains and pumps for obtaining drinking water are still relatively common sights, but few are as ornate as those to be seen at LINLITHGOW, West Lothian. The best known is St Michael's Well, named after the carving on the well-head of the town's patron saint – St Michael. Dated 1720, it displays the friendly-sounding motto adopted by the town: 'Saint Michael is Kinde to Straingers.'

The Cross Well, with ornate figures and unicorn on top, dates only from about 1806, but it is a remarkable copy of the original sixteenth-century well-head. The mason who undertook these elaborate carvings, Robert Gray, had only one hand. His other one had been cut off in an accident, forcing him to work with a mallet strapped to the stump.

The third well must have been the most popular for drinking from as it had the distinction of periodically flowing with 'bluid-red' wine. This miraculous and no doubt welcome sight occurred in the courtyard of Linlithgow Palace during royal festivities. On such occasions the three-tiered fountain, superbly carved with figures and dating from the time of James V, gushed with wine.

Inscriptions, as well as carvings, are popular on wells. One by the A838 to the northeast of RHICONICH, Sutherland, shows that it is not just the inhabitants of Linlithgow who are kind to strangers. The well was placed there by Peter Lawson as a mark of gratitude to the local people for their hospitality during the time that he was surveying the road.

A well by the Gifford Water, near BOLTON, East Lothian, also has a message of gratitude, this time to an individual, Agnes Broun, mother of Robert Burns. She used this well after the family moved from Ayrshire to East Lothian. A tribute to her says:

> *To the mortal and immortal memory*
> *And in noble tribute to her*
> *Who not only gave a son to Scotland*
> *But to the whole world*
> *And whose own doctrines*
> *He preached to humanity*
> *That we might learn.*

Robert Burns' genius was clearly absent when the rhyme on a plaque in KIRKCUD-BRIGHT, Stewartry, was composed to commemorate a new source of water for the burgh in 1763. The somewhat uninspired lines state:

This fount not riches life supplies
And gives what nature here denies
Prosperity must surely bless
Saint Cuthbert's sons who purchased this.

The reference to St Cuthbert reflects that the first church established here was dedicated to the saint – hence the town's name.

The strangely named Wilcebe Road on the Glentanar Estate, south of **ABOYNE**, Kincardine & Deeside, refers to the initials of a colourful former laird, William Cunliffe Brooks. He had a passion for providing and inscribing wells along this road. One such well warns: 'The worm of the still is the deadliest worm on the hill' – a reference to the dangers of drinking the potent, locally made illicit whisky. Presumably the exhortation to 'Drink, Thank, Think' is meant to refer to the local water, rather than the local 'water of life' or whisky. WCB also could not resist a pun or two. One well proclaims: 'Well to know when you are well off.'

An even more zany inscription about water is to be seen on a horse trough, originally in Guild Street, **ABERDEEN**, but now in the Duthie Winter Garden. It brashly proclaims:

Water springs for man and beast
Your service I am here
Although six thousand years of age
I am caller, clean and clear
– FOR THE INHABITANTS OF THE WORLD.

No doubt the inhabitants are all truly thankful for this magnificent gesture!

ABERDEEN seems to specialise in eccentricities connected with water. In FOOTDEE, near the North Pier, there is a peculiar water tap in the shape of a human-like face. Since the face has a tap sticking out of its mouth, the expression on it is understandably somewhat pained.

More tastefully designed, but nonetheless ornate, conveyors of water, can be seen in the shape of some nineteenth-century water towers, built to house a burgh's water cistern. The true function was sometimes cleverly disguised by means of an imposing neo-classical building in the case of PERTH, Perth & Kinross. The classical touch includes disguising the chimney of the pump house engine as a Roman triumphal column and placing a large Greek urn on top of it.

HEALING WELLS

Since pure water makes a positive contribution to health, it is only a short step to associating wells with cures for illnesses. The early Christian missionaries seem, shrewdly, to have adopted sites of pagan worship and ritual and then dedicated them to a Christian saint. This ensured the local people were not alienated by attacks on their customs, and allowed the church to claim any credit for subsequent cures at these traditional sites.

The more miraculous the cure the more likely, it was reasoned, that the water came from a holy well. Such places became centres of pilgrimage. WHITEKIRK, East Lothian, had such a well and one claim suggests over

14,500 people visited it in 1413. Hostels had to be built to house all the pilgrims, one of whom, in 1453, was a papal legate named Aeneas Sylvius. This man later became Pope, but must have forever regretted his visit to Whitekirk because it was detrimental to his health. Being used to the sunny climes of Italy, and not appreciating the bracing effects of the cooler Scottish air, he rashly chose to walk barefoot from the coast inland to White-kirk. The legate's legacy from this trip was to suffer from rheumatism ever after.

Although this well has now dried up, a superbly preserved mediaeval well, pre-dating the Reformation, can still be seen not far away at STENTON, East Lothian. It is housed within a cylindrical stone structure, with a conical roof topped by a stone shaped like a cardinal's hat.

Wells seem to have specialised in curing particular ailments. For instance, children would be taken to St Fillan's Well near KILMACOLM, Renfrew, to be cured of rickets, and to St Peter's Well in the Dropping Cave near the MULL OF LOGAN, Wigtown, for relief from whooping-cough. St Serf's Well at MONZIEVAIRD, Perth & Kinross, was the place for those with bladder trouble.

Sometimes the water had to be taken, not from a well, but from where it collected in a special rock. This was the case with the whooping-cough stone, or Clach'n Dru'chasd, at STRUAN, Perth & Kinross To complicate matters further, the water had to be drunk from a spoon made out of the horn from a living cow. The measles stone, or Clach a'

Ghriuthaich, near **FEARNAN**, Perth & Kinross, is chair-shaped. Children used to have their faces bathed in the healing water that collects in the hollow of the seat.

HEALING STONES

Very rarely it was the stones themselves, rather than the water they collected, which had the power to heal. The most remarkable of such stones are St Fillan's healing stones, which are now safely housed in the Tourist Information Centre at **KILLIN**, Stirling. These eight stones are said to have been consecrated by St Fillan himself in the eighth century. Each is associated with a particular part of the body. The cure is said to work by rubbing the appropriate stone on the afflicted area – three times one way, three times the other and then three times the first way again, accompanied by a Gaelic benediction. One attraction of such treatment, in today's financial climate, is that it is considerably cheaper than a course of drugs.

Just over the hills, to the north of Killin, is another stone associated both with healing and an early Christian missionary. In AD 664, Eonan – better known as St Adamnan – used his formidable powers of prayer to halt the spread of plague up **GLEN LYON**, Perth & Kinross, although he was astute enough to first send all the healthy people away up to the shielings at the head of the glen. The exact spot where the plague was checked is near **MILTON EONAN** – it is marked by a stone with what is said to be Eonan's cross carved on it.

Another stone in Glen Lyon, known as Am Bhacain or the Dog Stake, also had the power to ward off a particular and unwanted event. It is so named because the top of the stone resembles the head of a dog. In the eighteenth century it served as the local family planning clinic. It was common practice for local girls to crawl under the head to avoid unwanted pregnancies. Quite how this improbable contraceptive device worked is unclear, but the stone can still be found near CAMUSVRACHAN.

Stones could sometimes end up being a health risk if carelessly used. At a few places – such as CASHLIE in Glen Lyon, OLD DAILLY churchyard in Kyle & Carrick, and on the ISLE OF COLONSAY, near the golf course – large stones are to be found that were used as tests of virility. It was considered an impressive proof of manhood to lift these stones, but such a practice held the risk of injury. One man from the Isle of Gigha actually died after rupturing himself when trying to lift the Clach Thogolaich, or Lifting Stone, on the Isle of Colonsay. This led to the owner of Colonsay ordering the stone to be buried. However, old habits die hard and it was not long before the stone reappeared.

At other places, pieces of cloth rather than stones were critical to the medical process. At St Boniface's Well near MUNLOCHY, Ross & Cromarty, it was customary for those seeking help to hang up a piece of clothing on a near-by tree or bush before taking the water; the logic behind this idea being that the illness would transfer to the garment and rot away.

The advent of imperishable man-made fibres has clearly hindered rather than helped the healing process.

The first Sunday in May was the most popular time for activity at the 'Cloutie Wells', although modern visitors arrive at any time. The presence of this well is advertised by the odd sight of hundreds of motley bits of cloth and rags, including tea towels, J-cloths, underwear and outerwear, ties and tights, shirts and socks – festooning wire fences, over-hanging trees and overgrown banks for thirty yards on each side of the well. The array of items now hanging up gives the site all the character of a junk stall, rather than a holy well.

Sometimes money, rather than rags, was left as an offering. On the island of INNIS MAREE in Loch Maree, Ross & Cromarty, it was customary to hammer a coin into an oak tree by the holy well. Even Queen Victoria indulged in this, knocking in coins with a hammer specially brought over for the occasion, on her visit in 1877. This tradition may have been good for the health of the visitors, but it did not do much for the health of the oak tree. The unfortunate tree has succumbed to copper poisoning.

Items were sometimes left at wells to benefit animals as well as people. At the Slot Well, west of DALBEATTIE, Stewartry, shackles and other fittings worn by animals, such as oxen, were left by the well. In return some water was taken back for any sick animal to drink.

MEDICAL PRACTICES

Doctors gradually came to replace saints, stones and bits of cloth as the source of cures, although the rudimentary knowledge of medicine until relatively recent times meant traditional methods retained their popularity.

Probably the best known of the mediaeval medical families were the Beatons, who were physicians initially to the Lord of the Isles and later to the MacLeans of Duart on Mull. There is a memorial cairn and cross at PENNYGHAEL, Isle of Mull. In the fifteenth century they published their *Rule of Health*, which has been translated from the original Gaelic. Apart from being skilled in the use of herbs, they were far-sighted in stressing the need for a sensible diet, hygiene and exercise – now all in fashion in the late twentieth century.

Before breakfast, the Beatons advised stretching the arms and chest, having a good, clean spit, scrubbing sweat from the skin, washing hands and face, cleaning teeth, a prayer and good exercise. It is hard to fault such wisdom. They also advised having only three substantial meals in two days and before a heavy meal it was prudent to eat a roasted apple to relax the 'red humours'. Certain foods were to be treated with caution because 'great injury is caused by the raw things such as the oysters, and the things half raw as are the birds that are badly roasted'. Concerns about salmonella and badly-cooked poultry are not just a recent phenomena.

Less skilled medical practitioners than the

Beatons often ended up killing, rather than curing, their patients – as the unfortunate Donald Robertson found to his cost. According to his gravestone in ESHANESS churchyard, Shetland Isles, his death was caused ' … by the stupidity of Laurence Tulloch of Clothister who sold him nitre instead of Epsom salts by which he was killed in the space of five hours after taking a dose of it'.

The practice of applying leeches, which inject patients with a blood-thinning substance, used to be a popular medical treatment. In the first half of the nineteenth century, the White Loch of Ravenstone, south-west of SORBIE, Wigtown, was renowned for 'leeches of a superior sort'. The exciting task of collecting these friendly little creatures provided a source of income to people known as gill-gatherers. These were often elderly women who had to wade into the cold water ' … with their coats kilted high. The vampires lay hold of them by the legs, then the gill-gatherers take them off, and bottle them up'.

Although the Presbyterian church had no qualms about seeking cures by leeches, this tolerance did not extend to those who resorted to healing wells. In 1628, for instance, the Kirk Session at Falkirk pronounced:

> … if any person be found superstitiously and idolatrously, after this, to have passed in pilgrimage to Christ's Well, on Sundays of May, to seek their health, they shall repent in 'sacco' and linen three several Sabbaths and pay twenty lib. for ilk fault.

Despite such threats, it is clear that folk were still paying clandestine visits to ancient healing sites well into the nineteenth century. No doubt if all else had failed, it made sense to try the traditional cures. Modern research has, after all, revealed that they sometimes had a scientific basis.

What the seventeenth century Church would have made of modern spas is not clear, but the difference in function between a spa and an ancient healing well is not immediately apparent. During the nineteenth century, STRATHPEFFER, Ross & Cromarty, developed into a major spa town – 'Scotland's answer to the Bavarian watering place'. An impressive array of elegant Victorian hotels and ornamented villas were built there on a wooded hillside, to serve the flourishing tourist trade.

Spas, unlike old healing wells, cater largely for the rich, but at Strathpeffer the poor were able to sample the waters in the small Pump Room, built in 1839. Amazingly there was even an 'Institution for Poor Spa Drinkers'.

TROUBLE *at* WELL

Sometimes all was not well at a well. When taking the water involved actually bathing in an icy well, the effect was likely to do more harm than good, as Robert Burns found to his cost. Just before he died in 1796, he resorted to the waters of the Brow Well near RUTH-WELL, Nithsdale, and this can only have hastened his death. On other occasions wells have, deliberately rather than inadvertently, been used to kill people. St Patrick's Well near **KIRKPATRICK-DURHAM**, Stewartry, lost its healing properties after a mother drowned her child in it.

Drowning was the method of execution favoured by the Picts and it is very likely that the impressive well at **BURGHEAD**, Moray, was used for this purpose. This well, dating from Pictish times, is fully enclosed and cut out of solid rock. It is approached down twenty steps, also cut into rock, and entered in a dramatic fashion through a black hole beneath a grassy slope. The Pictish cross-slab at **GLAMIS**, Angus, appears to portray such an execution by drowning. It shows a large cauldron into which two victims have been plunged. Their legs can be seen sticking out the top.

Perhaps the well that is most associated with a murder is the Well of the Heads, south of Invergarry beside Loch Oich, **INVERNESS**. It can be identified by a tall pyramid with seven heads around its top. In 1663 the young heir to the chieftainship of the MacDonalds of Keppoch and his two brothers were murdered by rivals to the title. The clan bard, Iain Lom, obtained permission from the chief of the neighbouring MacDonalds of Glengarry to hunt down the killers. This task was accomplished and the rest of the story is told on the sides of the monument:

> *The heads of the seven murderers were presented at the feet of the noble chief in Glengarry Castle after having been washed in this spring, and ever since that event, which took place in the early 16th century it has been known as Tobar-nan-Ceann, or Well of the Heads.*

Unfortunately, the chief of Glengarry, who erected the column in 1812, seems to have had only a hazy knowledge of his family history since the inscription refers to the wrong century and hence to the wrong chief who ensured that justice was done.

A fight, rather than a murder, is portrayed on a well in **NORTH QUEENSFERRY**, Dunfermline. The plaque depicts a struggle between a local fishwife and a visiting sailor, although at first glance the picture seems to be portraying a dance rather than a fight. Since the village well was the only source of fresh water, it had to be used sparingly – especially during dry weather. To protect their water, the local fishwives were quite prepared to resort to their fish gutting knives in a bid to drive away outsiders, such as uninvited sailors.

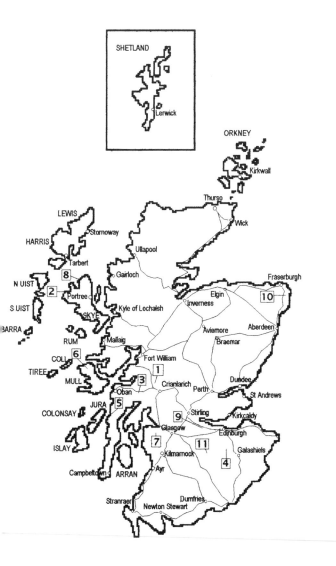

SHETLAND

Lerwick

ORKNEY

Kirkwall

Thurso

Wick

LEWIS

Stornoway

HARRIS

Ullapool

Tarbert

Gairloch

8

N UIST

2

Portree

S UIST

Kyle of Lochalsh

SKYE

Fraserburgh

Elgin

Inverness

10

Aviemore

Braemar

Aberdeen

BARRA

RUM

COLL

6

TIREE

MULL

Mallaig

Fort William

1

Oban

3

Crianlarich

Perth

Dundee

St Andrews

COLONSAY

JURA

5

Stirling

Kirkcaldy

9

Glasgow

Edinburgh

7

ISLAY

Kilmarnock

11

Galashiels

4

Campbeltown

ARRAN

Ayr

Stranraer

Newton Stewart

Dumfries

MAP 4 — MAKING MERRY

MAKING MERRY

Ref	Location	Description
1	Beinn Dorain	Mountain praised by Duncan Ban
2	Borreraig	Cairn on site of piping college
3	Dalmally	Duncan Ban MacIntyre's memorial
4	Dewar's Gill	Piper's grave
5	Duntrune Castle	Ghostly piper
6	Glenbellart, Mull	Bard writing of clearances
7	Kilbarchan	Habbie Simpson's statue
8	Kilmuir	Gravestone of piper, Charles MacKarter
9	Linlithgow	Carved drummers
10	Longside	Jamie Fleeman's grave
11	Skirling	Sad piper

MAKING MERRY: MUSIC AND ENTERTAINMENT

Musicians and entertainers were employed by burghs for official and public functions, and by lairds for their own private entertainment. Pipers generally had a prominent role when it came to clan battles, the emotive skirl of the pipes being able to rouse even the most placid of clansmen to fierce fury.

Banging the DRUM

Many burghs employed an official drummer to undertake those functions which required the 'tuck of drum'. These included summoning local citizens to public occasions – such as to witness a punishment – publicising special announcements, and acting as an alarm-clock by noisily waking everyone up at an anti-social early hour like four in the morning. Who woke the drummer up first is not clear.

Sadly very few reminders of their existence are evident in Scotland today, but two notable exceptions are still to be found at LINLITHGOW, West Lothian. Both are small carved stone figures on fountains.

The older, dating from about 1520 and much worn with age, is on the elaborate structure within the courtyard of the Palace. The more recent and better preserved of the drummers is a mere 190 years old, and is to be seen banging his drum on the Cross Well.

Paying the PIPER

Instead of employing a drummer, a burgh might choose to maintain a piper for both ceremonial occasions and lighter entertainment. One of the piper's tasks was to summon council members to meetings, as well as to provide music at festive occasions. Not everyone appreciated the talents of the piper. In 1676 a visitor to Scotland, Thomas Kirke, complained, 'Musick they have, but not the harmony of the sphears, but loud terrene noises like the bellowing of beasts; the loud bagpipe is their chief delight'.

Pipers frequently seem to have been colourful characters, all too fond of a dram

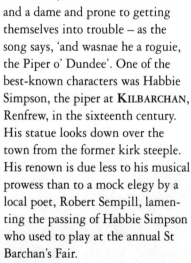

and a dame and prone to getting themselves into trouble – as the song says, 'and wasnae he a roguie, the Piper o' Dundee'. One of the best-known characters was Habbie Simpson, the piper at KILBARCHAN, Renfrew, in the sixteenth century. His statue looks down over the town from the former kirk steeple. His renown is due less to his musical prowess than to a mock elegy by a local poet, Robert Sempill, lamenting the passing of Habbie Simpson who used to play at the annual St Barchan's Fair.

In contrast, an older, sadder and unknown stone piper, dating, it appears, from 1415, glares rather than stares through melancholy black eyes out on the village of SKIRLING, Tweeddale.

Another anonymous piper is commemorated in the Borders by a stone marking 'The Piper's Grave' at DEWAR'S GILL, Tweeddale. The story is that this piper took bets in a bar at Peebles as to the distance he could walk playing his pipes. Excess drink, no doubt, encouraged him to exaggerate his ability and he ended up intending to walk all the way to Lauder, a distance of 25 miles. Not surprisingly this proved over-ambitious, and his task was made even more difficult by faulty navigation which took him away from the shortest route, probably because all those accompanying him were equally befuddled by their liquid refreshments. The effort of piping and walking proved too much and at the top of the pass above Glentress, having covered twelve miles, the exhausted piper collapsed and died.

In the Highlands and Islands the clan chiefs maintained their hereditary pipers. Pipe music was taught in colleges of piping and passed on from generation to generation. The traditional stronghold of piping was on the Isle of Skye where both the MacDonalds and MacLeods maintained hereditary pipers. The MacArthurs were pipers to the MacDonald chiefs at Duntulm Castle and one of their number, Charles, is buried at KILMUIR. His eighteenth century gravestone notes that his 'fame as an honest man and a remarkable piper will survive this generation'.

The most famous pipers of all time, the MacCrimmons, were maintained at Dunvegan Castle by the chief of the MacLeods. They were the hereditary pipers to the MacLeods for ten generations between about 1500 and 1800 and had their renowned college of piping at **BORRERAIG**, Skye. Other clan chiefs sent their own pipers to this college for instruction in the classical pipe tunes. The Gaelic on the memorial cairn near the site notes that the MacCrimmons were 'renowned as Composers, Performers and Instructors of the classical bagpipe music or piobaireachd'. The piping course lasted three years and to complete it a student was required to memorise 195 classical compositions.

One of the most outstanding and moving tunes was composed by one Donald Ban MacCrimmon just before he left, apparently reluctantly, with his chief to join the government forces opposing Bonnie Prince Charlie.

Donald sensed that he would not return and he composed what became known as 'Cumhna MhicCriomain' or 'MacCrimmon's Lament'. During the ill-fated MacLeod expedition, Donald was captured by the Duke of Huntly's forces. Next morning none of the pipers with the Duke's forces was willing to play. Enquiring as to the reason, the Duke was told it was because the great MacCrimmon was their prisoner. Unwilling to upset his pipers, the Duke immediately released Donald. But not long afterwards, in a skirmish known as the Rout of Moy, Donald was killed.

Although no pipers remain at Borreraig, some of their number continue to frequent sites formerly associated with them. One such place is **DUNTRUNE CASTLE** on Loch Crinan, Argyll & Bute. This was the scene of a bloody episode in 1644 following the invasion of Argyll by Colkitto MacDonald and his supporters. They planned to attack Duntrune and their piper was sent on ahead to gather information. He was admitted to the castle by the unsuspecting garrison, but his questions and actions subsequently aroused suspicions. As a result he was confined to a room in one of the turrets. In the distance he saw the war galleys of the MacDonalds coming up the loch. Knowing the garrison were alerted, he took up his pipes and played a tune, which became known as the 'Piper's Warning to his Master'. Like all self-respecting pipers he could make his pipes speak. The MacDonalds, heeding the message, called off the attack. The infuriated garrison hurried up the stairs and cut off the piper's fingers. He died from shock and loss of blood and was buried within the castle. His ghost continued to haunt the castle, although recent exorcisms seem to have quietened his restless soul.

BARDIC VERSES

Highland clan chiefs often maintained a retinue consisting of harpist, bard and jester, as well as a piper. The last MacLeod chief to do so was Iain Breac, who succeeded to the title in 1664. Bards are closely associated with the rich Gaelic oral traditions of the Highlands and Islands and generally held pride of place amongst a Highland chief's cultural entourage. The MacMhurich family were the hereditary bards to the Lords of the Isles and would have been able to recite all the relevant genealogy, as well as colourful stories passed on from lip to ear over the generations. In the absence of written records the bards were the custodians of a clan's history.

With the break-up of the clan system which followed the disaster of Culloden, the traditional bards disappeared as the Gaelic aristocracy that patronised them became either Anglicised or sold their lands to outsiders. They were succeeded by a new breed of untrained poets with no allegiance to a particular clan chief.

Duncan Ban MacIntyre (yellow haired Duncan of the Songs), despite being illiterate, became one of the most celebrated and colourful of these later Gaelic bards. He was born near Loch Tulla in 1724, but died in 1812 in Edinburgh. There is a rather inelegant monument to him, a cross between Stonehenge and a Greek temple, on a hill above DALMALLY, Argyll & Bute.

Duncan's poetic abilities were stimulated by a dispute. A neighbour persuaded Duncan to go in his stead to join the forces being assembled from the Campbell lands to oppose the Jacobites under Bonnie Prince Charlie. He gave Duncan his sword and a promise of money when the campaign was over. Duncan found he was neither sufficiently belligerent nor sufficiently anti-Jacobite to enjoy the experience. He managed to lose his neighbour's sword in his first bout of fighting and decided it would be far more sensible to leave others to carry on the battle. On returning home, he sought the payment promised by his neighbour. The latter, however, was impressed neither by the loss of his sword, nor by Duncan's early return from the fray – so he refused to pay. Duncan felt aggrieved enough to compose a rude poem, whereupon his neighbour came round and beat him up.

Fortunately this unconventional way of paying for a piece of poetry failed to divert Duncan from his composing. In fact it seems that very little could divert him when he was in full creative flow. It is said that one day he was lying in bed thinking up a new poem, when the rain started to drip through the roof. Not to be deterred, he called out to his wife, Mairi, to suggest that she should go out and repair the thatch because water was coming in.

Duncan wrote poems for love not money and to support his wife and himself he became a gamekeeper on the Breadalbane estates around the Black Mount. His passion for both the local mountains and hunting deer figure prominently in his most renowned composition in praise of the shapely peak of BEINN DORAIN.

It was not only Duncan Ban MacIntyre who found that anger was a spur to poetry. A number of the Gaelic bards who witnessed the destruction of their culture and society with the onset of the Highland Clearances wrote movingly but bitterly about what they saw.

English translations can only give some indication of the depth of their feelings. On the Isle of Mull, the situation was summed up by Angus MacMhuirich:

The land of our love lies under bracken and
  heather,
every plain and every field untilled
and soon there will be none in Mull of the Trees
but Lowlanders and their white sheep.

This prophecy proved all too true. Ruined townships that were cleared of their inhabitants can be seen throughout the island and good examples occur in **GLENBELLART** to the south of Dervaig. Today Mull supports only a small population, many of whom are incomers, and the Gaelic language is rarely heard.

Jest a MINUTE

Whereas the names of poets from the past are often well known, this is rarely the case with jesters. This is a real contrast to nowadays when comedians are generally better known than poets. Probably the most famous jester was Jamie Fleeman (or Fleming) who lived between 1713 and 1779. He was very quick-witted. When an arrogant visitor enquired, 'Whose fool are you?', Jamie responded, 'I'm the Laird o' Udny's fool. Whose fool are *you?*'

Once when he was leading a donkey, an attempt to gain a laugh at his expense back-fired when a bystander mocked, 'Is that your brother, Jamie?' Quick as a flash Jamie replied, 'No, just an acquaintance like yourself'.

On another occasion his quick thinking served to save not savage. The Laird of Udny's house caught fire in 1734, but the family were rescued thanks to Jamie.

Inappropriately, he is best remembered for a sad comment. When dying he said, 'Dinna bury me like a beast' – a phrase inscribed on his tombstone at LONGSIDE, Banff & Buchan.

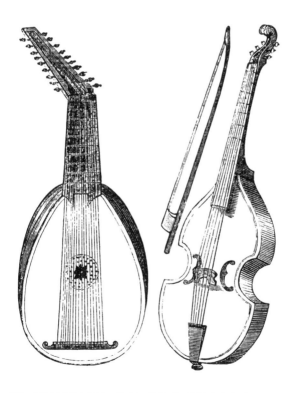

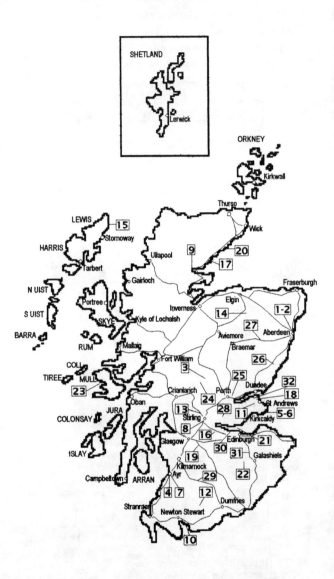

MAP 5 – BRIDGE THAT GAP

BRIDGE THAT GAP

Ref	Location	Description
1	Aberdeen	Old Bridge of Dee
2	Aberdeen	Brig o' Balgonie
3	Aberfeldy	Wade's military bridge
4	Alloway	Tam o' Shanter and witches
5	Anstruther Easter	Accident in Cunzie Burn
6	Anstruther Wester	Plaque – James V carried across Dreel burn
7	Ayr	Auld Brig's debate with New Brig
8	Bannockburn	Bridge built due to a splash
9	Bonar Bridge	Bridge with names of Parliamentary Commissioners
10	Creetown	Beardie's Bridge
11	Dairsie	Bridge built by Archbishop Beaton
12	Dalry	Bridge built by local tailor
13	Doune	Bridge built to spite ferryman
14	Dufftown	Disputed crossing
15	Garry, Lewis	Bridge built by Lord Leverhulme
16	Glen Village	Faces on bridge
17	Golspie	Parliamentary bridge
18	Guardbridge	Bridge with arms of Archbishop Beaton
19	Hamilton	Bridge built due to missed meeting
20	Helmsdale	Parliamentary bridge
21	Inchgarvie	Pillar of original Forth Rail Bridge
22	Innerleithen	Vacant stipend bridge

Ref	Location	Description
23	Isle of Ulva	Tariff for dogs
24	Kenmore	Bridge funded by forced land sales
25	Kinnoull	Ferryman on gravestone
26	Logie Pert	North Water Bridge
27	Potarch	Bridge destroyed by floated timber
28	Rumbling Bridge	Double bridge
29	Sanquhar	Glenairlie Bridge
30	South Queensferry	Forth Rail Bridge
31	Stow	Collection bridge
32	Wormit	Old Tay rail bridge

BRIDGE THAT GAP

FORDS *and* AFFORDABLE CROSSINGS

In earlier times rivers generally proved severe barriers to travel and had to be crossed by fords, by wading, by stepping stones or by ferry. The first three methods in particular had their dangers when the river was in spate, and loss of life was not uncommon.

In a few places an adventurous alternative was to cross a river on stilts. In the mid eighteenth century the inhabitants of Dollar, Clackmannan, were known for their prowess on stilts, and at Melrose, Ettrick & Lauderdale, stilts could be hired to cross the River Tweed.

In some areas local women used to carry people, for a fee, across the river on their backs. One such woman was well rewarded for her exertions. James V took to travelling around Scotland in disguise to elicit the views of his subjects. At ANSTRUTHER, North East Fife, he was reluctant to wet his clothes by wading across the Dreel burn and a 'stout gaberlunzie', or beggar woman, volunteered to carry him across. Her initiative paid off and she was rewarded with the King's purse – an event recorded by a plaque on the Dreel Tavern.

Ferries were usually a more comfortable way of crossing water, but since they were nearly always monopolies abuses sometimes occurred and regulations were imposed to cover fare levels, service frequency and safety aspects. The penalties introduced in an Act of 1551 threatened ferrymen who were guilty of overcharging with the forfeit not only of their goods, but also of their lives! (Caledonian MacBrayne be warned ....) There is a rare portrayal of a ferryman and his boat on a gravestone at KINNOULL, Perth & Kinross, but his death had nothing to do with over-charging customers.

There is a nice touch of humour connected with the ferry to the ISLE OF ULVA, off Mull. A list of former tariffs to be seen in the church shows that a dog could travel free with its owner, but it was charged 3d if it was on its own. An appealing feature of the Ulva ferry is that it is still summoned in a traditional way. The attention of the ferryman on the island is attracted by moving a slat on a white board to reveal a red signal.

BRIDGES *over* TROUBLED WATERS

Bridges have been the setting for a range of tragedies – either because the bridge itself, or people on it, fell down. The Tay rail bridge is not only the longest in Britain, but is also associated with the country's most infamous rail disaster. On the stormy night of 28th December 1879, only 19 months after the bridge opened, its central girders collapsed as a train was crossing. The engine and coaches plunged into the icy waters of the Tay, with

The TAY BRIDGE, *before* DECEMBER 1879

the loss of all 85 passengers and crew. The inquiry blamed the designer, Thomas Bouch, for serious design flaws, as well as the builders, both for using poor quality materials and for faulty workmanship. A few years later Scotland's most renowned bad poet, William McGonagall, was sufficiently moved by the disaster to pen poetry that was excruciatingly awful even by his own standards. A brief example will suffice:

> *As soon as the catastrophe came to be known*
> *The alarm from mouth to mouth was blown,*
> *And the cry rang out all o'er the town,*
> *Good Heavens! the Tay Bridge is blown down.*

The replacement bridge, which opened in 1887, was built alongside its notorious predecessor, the piers of which are still clearly visible from **WORMIT**, North East Fife.

The effects of this tragic event have also left their mark on the world famous rail bridge across the River Forth. Thomas Bouch's plans had been accepted for the proposed new Forth railway bridge and preliminary construction work had started. One of the stone piers for his bridge can still be seen on the island of INCHGARVIE in the Forth, but it now supports only a lighthouse. Following the collapse of the Tay bridge, building work was halted, Bouch's plans were scrapped, the proposed crossing was reassessed and a new design commissioned from Sir John Fowler and Benjamin Baker. Their proposals for a cantilever and central girder design were developed into today's familiar and much loved Forth Rail Bridge, SOUTH QUEENSFERRY, Edinburgh. This Forth wonder of the world was completed in 1890.

Not everyone was impressed at the time. William Morris described it as 'the supremest specimen of all ugliness', which only goes to prove that one man's 'feat' is another man's poison! The new bridge was at the forefront of steel technology and design, but it was massively over-engineered as a reaction to the events on the Tay.

Bridges can be brought down by trees as well as trains, as the bridge at POTARCH, Kincardine & Deeside, found to its cost. In 1814, while still under construction, it was destroyed by timber being floated down the River Dee. It was of little consolation to the bridge to know that its demise led to an Act being passed to restrict timber-floating to the spring and summer when there is generally less water in the rivers.

When individuals rather than bridges fall, the damage can sometimes be self-inflicted. At Beardie's Bridge in CREETOWN, Wigtown, a local worthy by the name of James Connell decided he could use the bridge to launch himself to fame. He made himself wings out of sheepskin and hoops and then attempted to glide off the bridge. To the surprise of no one but himself, he ignominiously fell into the burn and broke his ankle.

Glenairlie Bridge near SANQUHAR, Nithsdale, was also the scene of a lucky escape for someone who, similarly, fell off as a result of his own stupidity. A plaque on the bridge, erected 'as a warning to disobedient youth of future generations', explains that a horse, frightened by a train, jumped over the parapet and was drowned in the river below. The young rider, bringing the horse back from having it shod at the Mennock Smithy, had ignored strict instructions to *lead* the horse and not to ride it. He 'miraculously survived' – at least until the farmer who owned the horse got hold of him!

In marked contrast, those crossing the river at RUMBLING BRIDGE, Perth & Kinross, went to great trouble to avoid falling off. The structure, built in 1713, is unusual in that though it is narrow and 86 feet above a rocky burn, there are no parapets. Such an inducement to vertigo, not surprisingly, made the bridge unpopular with travellers, and coach passengers took to walking or even crawling across the bridge rather than staying in their vehicle. This naturally limited its appeal to customers – and hence to turnpike road operators – so a new bridge was built directly above the older one in 1816. Although the drop to the river is further – 120 feet – the greater width and presence of parapets removed the previous sense of exposure and left Rumbling Bridge with a unique and impressive double bridge.

There is also an impressive double connected, literally, with the bridge over the Union Canal near GLEN VILLAGE, Falkirk. Its distinguishing feature is a pair of heads. On one parapet there is a head with a smiling face and on the other a head with a very mournful face. The former looks back on the newly dug section of the canal coming from Edinburgh, whereas the latter looks forward only to the hardships that could be expected when the next section of the canal was cut because it involved constructing a tunnel.

The faces of David Maver and the wife of John McInnes were far from happy when they ended up in Dullan Water near DUFFTOWN, Moray, as a result of a local feud. Between 1727 and 1770 the local wooden bridge was repeatedly washed away. When it was decided to seek a new site a dispute broke out as to whose land it should be on, since it would benefit the landowner concerned. A tree trunk was pressed into action as a makeshift bridge and it was this that Mr Maver and Mrs McInnes were negotiating en route to church. The servant of Mr McGregor, one of the land-owners disputing the site for the new bridge, knocked the tree trunk and threw the couple into the river. Mrs McInnes, however, was not a woman to be trifled with. She clambered out of the water and set about the servant, pulling his hair and beating him over the head with a stick. She continued on her way to church, but afterwards 'complained of abortion'. This skirmish spurred Mr McGregor's opponents

to act, and equipping themselves with guns
as well as tools they replaced the tree trunk
with a proper bridge over the Dullan Water.

BRIDGES —
A THEME *for a* DREAM

Even bridges built as a result of a dream were
not immune from falling down, as John
Erskin discovered 400 years ago. He dreamed
that unless he built a bridge at a place called
Stormy Grain, he would be miserable after he
died. Since the name meant nothing to him,
the prospects for his happiness in the afterlife
did not look too promising. Fortunately his
problem was solved in an unexpected way. He
was walking by the River North Esk when he
happened to stop and pass the time of day
with an old lady. She fortuitously mentioned
that they were at a spot called Stormy Grain.
Duly thankful, he set to work building his
bridge, but his troubles were not yet over. The
bridge was washed away twice and the North
Water Bridge near LOGIE PERT, Angus, was
only completed at the third attempt.

A dream of bringing employment and
prosperity to a depressed area was the inspiration for building the bridge at GARRY on
the Isle of Lewis. It is an impressive concrete
structure, spanning a deep gorge, and built at
what must have been considerable expense.
The bridge has all the hallmarks of one leading to somewhere of importance. It comes as
a complete surprise, therefore, to find the
road ends immediately beyond the bridge.
This structure, like the dream of which it was

a part, sadly promises more than it delivers. Lord Leverhulme had it built on what was intended to be a new route to the north end of Lewis as part of his plans for developing the local fishing industry. Unfortunately circumstances conspired against him and his vision was never fulfilled. This far-sighted project was abandoned uncompleted, leaving a sad legacy of empty buildings, unfinished roads and this bridge to nowhere.

Another bridge associated with someone's imagination is the Auld Brig in AYR, Kyle & Carrick. Robert Burns in his poem 'The Twa Brigs' describes the abuse which he envisaged might be exchanged between the brash new bridge and its elderly neighbour. The latter is described by the new bridge as 'that poor narrow footpath of a street, where twa wheel-barrows tremble when they meet'. The prophetic response was, 'I'll be a brig when you're a shapeless cairn'. Although Burns could not know it, the new bridge was to be washed away in 1877. The Auld Brig still stands.

Burns also describes a bridge that, far from being associated with disaster, actually prevented one. In what is probably his best known poem, Robert Burns describes how Tam o' Shanter disturbed a coven of witches in the ruined kirk at Alloway. They pursued him and he was saved from their clutches only by the gallant efforts of his horse, Meg, who carried him to safety across the Auld Brig o' Doon at ALLOWAY, Kyle & Carrick. Witches are unable to cross running water, but before Meg reached the critical point of safety half-way across the river, one of the witches grabbed her tail and pulled it off. Meg's tail may have gone, but the bridge is still there.

Tam o' Shanter may have escaped disaster, but others were not so lucky. John Loch, a merchant in **ANSTRUTHER**, North East Fife, was on his way home from church when he heard a child had been drowned in the Cunzie Burn. Hurrying to the spot, he was horrified to discover it was his daughter. To prevent any similar tragedy in future, he paid for the burn to be covered by a causeway in 1721.

A succession of near disasters when crossing the Polharrow river near **DALRY**, Stewartry, persuaded Quintin McLurg, a local tailor, to pay for a bridge to be built so that others would not have to suffer similar nerve-racking encounters with the water.

Another tailor had a rather less alarming experience when fording a river. Robert Spittal, tailor to James IV, was splashed. This so upset him that, to avoid repetition, he built Spittal's Bridge at **BANNOCKBURN**, Stirling in 1516. To show the bridge was tailor-made he had a pair of scissors carved above the arch.

Robert Spittal possessed a prickly temperament and seems to have been easily displeased. If his ire was roused, he was inclined to turn to bridge-building. When the ferryman refused him passage across the River Teith, on the reasonable grounds that he had no money with him, Robert Spittal, in a fit of spite, vowed to put the man out of business by building a bridge. This he duly did in 1535 when the bridge at **DOUNE**, Stirling, was completed.

ANSWERS *to* PRAYERS

Since an impassable river provided an acceptable excuse for people not to attend church on a Sunday, the Kirk Session had an incentive to provide a bridge, no doubt to the dismay of some of their less conscientious parishioners. Special fund-raising collections were organised by the Session and a spate of these 'collection bridges' were built in the seventeenth century. To reduce costs, such bridges were only built wide enough for people and horses. A superb 3-arched example of such a narrow bridge is at STOW, Ettrick & Lauderdale. It was funded out of collections made in 1654 and 1655.

Another way for the Session to pay for a bridge was to turn any vacancy for a minister to advantage. The money potentially available to pay a minister could be used for good works including bridge building. The Cuddy Bridge at INNERLEITHEN, Tweeddale, completed in 1697, was funded out of such a vacant stipend. The local people may have temporarily lost a minister, but they permanently gained a bridge.

It was not just the Presbyterian Church that was active in bridge building. Prior to the Reformation, the Catholic Church had also been busy. Particularly attractive examples, dating from 1520 to 1540, are the old bridges across the River Dee in ABERDEEN, built by Bishop Dunbar, and at GUARDBRIDGE and DAIRSIE in North East Fife, built by Archbishop Beaton. Though it may be more blessed to give than to receive, these bridge-building bishops believed in publicising their munificence by displaying their arms and initials on their bridges. Clearly if there were any blessings going, they intended to ensure they were not forgotten!

Charitable motives or thoughts of blessings were far from the mind of another churchman when he paid for a bridge to be built over the Avon Water near **HAMILTON**. A local priest had determined that his view would prevail when a particularly controversial matter came to be debated by churchmen at a gathering in Hamilton. On the day in question he set out with a large number of supporters, but the river was in such spate that they were unable to cross. As a result his rivals carried the day. Such was his anger that he built the bridge to ensure that he would not be thwarted in this way again.

Sometimes these bridges built by churchmen survive thanks only to the later generosity of laymen. The Brig o' Balgonie across the River Don in **ABERDEEN** was originally built in 1329 by Henry Cheyne, the Bishop of Aberdeen. Upkeep was a problem until 1605 when Sir Alexander Hay endowed a fund for its maintenance out of the feu duties from his properties. These property investments were indeed so successful that other bridges were subsequently funded from these feus, including the new Bridge of Don, built in 1850.

BRIDGES *built by soldiering on*

Not all individuals responsible for funding bridges contributed on a voluntary basis. Following the 1745 Jacobite rising, the estates

of many of the more ardent supporters of
Bonnie Prince Charlie's ill-fated escapade were
confiscated by the government. Some of the
money raised by selling this land was used to
build bridges. The one at **KENMORE**, Perth &
Kinross, dating from 1774, has a plaque
stating that 'His Majesty gave in aid to it
out of the annexed estates £1000'.

The Jacobite rebellions of 1715 and 1745
gave a spur to bridge building in other ways
too. The outbreak of unrest led to the government's funding a network of military roads
and associated bridges in the Highlands.
General Wade built about 40 bridges, with a
further 938 being constructed by his military
successors, such as Major Caulfeild. The most
impressive of all is Wade's five-arched bridge
at **ABERFELDY**, Perth & Kinross. It was
designed by William Adam, ornamented with
four obelisks, and opened in 1733. The
English inscription explains it was erected
'for securing a safe and easy communication
between the high lands and the tradeing [sic]
towns of the low country'. Its Latin counterpart is more colourful, at least insofar as it
has been interpreted by Latin scholars. It
grandly proclaims:

> *Admire this military road stretching on this
> side and that 250 miles beyond the limits of
> the Roman one, mocking moors and bogs,
> opened up through rocks and over mountains,
> and, as you see, crossing the indignant Tay.*

Local highland chiefs, apparently, were
less enthusiastic about such new bridges,

taking the view that they would 'render the ordinary people effeminate' if they no longer had to wade across rivers.

Military bridges were succeeded by Parliamentary bridges in the Highlands. Between 1803 and 1828 an impressive total of 1117 such bridges were funded by the government and built under the supervision of the outstanding engineer Thomas Telford, in a bid to improve social and economic conditions in the area. Fine examples of such bridges survive at **HELMSDALE** and **GOLSPIE**, Sutherland. At **BONAR BRIDGE**, Sutherland, the original plaque, dated 1815, has been transferred to the later bridge. It demands:

> *Traveller Stop and Read with Gratitude the names of the Parliamentary Commissioners appointed in the Year 1803 to direct the making of above Five Hundred miles of Roads through the Highlands of Scotland and of numerous bridges … connecting those roads.*

As with the bishops before them, the Parliamentary Commissioners were anxious to ensure their names were not forgotten by posterity. In fact they were so keen on this that two later Commissioners even went to the length of ensuring that their names 'were afterwards added' to the original list of seven shown on the plaque.

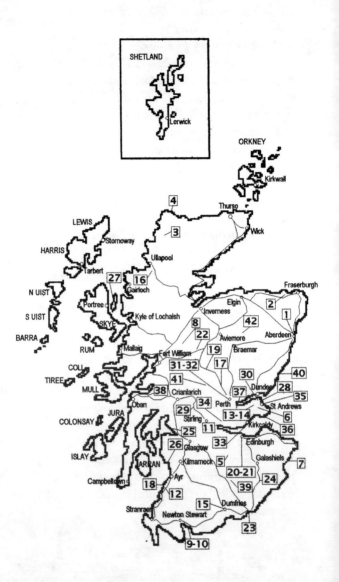

SHETLAND

Lerwick

ORKNEY

Kirkwall

Thurso

Wick

4

3

LEWIS

Stornoway

HARRIS

Ullapool

Tarbert

27

16

Gairloch

N UIST

Portree

S UIST

SKYE

Kyle of Lochalsh

Inverness

Elgin

Fraserburgh

2

1

42

Aberdeen

BARRA

RUM

Mallaig

8

22

Aviemore

Braemar

19

Fort William

COLL

TIREE

MULL

38

31-32

17

30

Dundee

40

28

35

41

Crianlarich

37

Perth

St Andrews

Oban

29

34

13-14

6

Stirling

JURA

COLONSAY

25

11

Kirkcaldy

36

26

Glasgow

33

Edinburgh

ISLAY

ARRAN

Kilmarnock

5

Galashiels

7

Campbeltown

18

Ayr

20-21

24

39

12

15

Dumfries

Stranraer

Newton Stewart

23

9-10

MAP 6 — TAKE THE HIGH ROAD

TAKE THE HIGH ROAD

Ref	Location	Description
1	Aberdeen	Road to bankruptcy
2	Aberdour	Jane Whyte's memorial
3	Achfary	Black and white telephone kiosk
4	Balnakeil	Highwayman's gravestone
5	Carnwath	Ayr mis-spelt
6	Ceres	Plaque to balloon trip
7	Coldstream	Toll House
8	Corrieyairack Pass	Wade Road
9	Creetown	Tank Road
10	Creetown	Milestone pointing wrong way
11	Culross	Croun o' the causey
12	Culroy	Old AA plaque
13	Cupar	Tollhouse
14	Cupar	Milestone with 1/7 mile
15	Dumfries	Mid Steeple mileplate
16	Dundonnell	Destitution Road
17	Dunkeld	Tollhouse at centre of 1868 riots
18	Dunure	Electric Brae
19	Edendon Bridge	Wade's Stone
20	Edinburgh	Link snuffer
21	Edinburgh	Post Chaise milestone
22	Garvamore	Original King's House
23	Gretna	Sark Toll House
24	Hawick	Victorian letterbox warning
25	Helensburgh	Highway to matrimony
26	Irvine	Coach crash
27	Isle of Raasay	Calum's Road
28	Kincaple	Tollhouse and bar at 6 mile mark

Ref	Location	Description
29	Kingshouse	Milestone with 0 miles
30	Newport-on-Tay	Milestone with 0 miles
31	Perth	Tollhouse with tariff board
32	Perth	Notice on Perth Bridge re red flag
33	Pettycur	Names on milestones
34	Rumbling Bridge	Milestone with wrong distance
35	St Andrews	Monument to Archbishop Sharp
36	St Monans	Milestone with individual buildings
37	Strathmiglo	Right of way through inn
38	Taynuilt	The Farewell Stone
39	Tweedshaws	Memorial cairn to mail coachmen
40	Usan	Coastguard watchtower
41	Weem	General Wade's picture
42	Well of the Lecht	Stone plaque erected by 33rd Regiment

A MOUNTAIN PASS *in the* GRAMPIANS

TAKE
THE
HIGH ROAD

All BUILDERS
GREAT *and* SMALL

Roads have often been constructed in response
to crises of a national or local nature. There
have been a sufficient number of these in the
past two centuries to have given quite a boost
to road building. For example, the consternation induced by the Jacobite rebellion of
1715, which started in the Highlands, led to
the building of a network of military roads in
the area to allow troops to be moved in at the
first sign of trouble.

The first and best known of the military
road builders was General Wade, who was
appointed by the government in 1724. One
of the few pictures of him can be seen on the
front of the inn at WEEM, Perth & Kinross.
Underneath is written: 'Here in the year 1733
General Wade Soldier and Engineer lived'.

The ordinary soldiers were billeted not in
inns, but out in buildings referred to as 'King's
Houses', so-called because they were built
alongside the King's Highway. A rare example
of one of the original King's Houses can still
be seen at GARVAMORE, Inverness.

The most dramatic surviving stretch of a
Wade road is seen between the head of Loch
Ness and the upper reaches of the River Spey.
There the road crosses the CORRIEYAIRACK

PASS, Inverness, and zig-zags through 13 hair-pin bends up to a height of 2500 feet. This route is spectacular, but represents one of the few misjudgments made by Wade. On this occasion he seems to have underestimated the difficulties of using the road during a Highland winter. Not surprisingly, later roads sought out a totally different route – lower and less exposed.

Since it was not uncommon for the new roads to be snow-bound in winter, marker stones were frequently placed alongside them to show their alignment. One of these markers, standing about six feet in height, inscribed with the date 1729 and known as Wade's Stone, has been carefully preserved alongside the new A9 road to the north west of EDEN-DON BRIDGE, Perth & Kinross. It is said that when no one was looking Wade reached up and put a gold guinea piece on top of the stone. When he returned the following year it was still there whereupon Wade, who was Irish, is reputed to have pointed this out to his English troops and, referring to the local inhabitants, remarked: 'True, they may be bare-arsed, but there's not a one that isn't honest. I could not have done that in your country, gentlemen!'

Another roadside legacy, dating from the era of Major Caulfeild, Wade's successor, can be found beside the Cockbridge to Tomintoul road. At the WELL OF THE LECHT, Moray, a white stone plaque, dated 1754 and inscribed in crude script, records that five companies from the 33rd Regiment made the road from here to the Spey. This simple memorial belies the herculean task that had been accomplished by unskilled soldiers across difficult terrain and in a hostile climate.

A modern military road, the 'Tank Road', can be seen near CREETOWN, Wigtown. This white concrete road was hurriedly laid down in the early 1940s to carry the weight of tanks being driven from their unloading point at Creetown station to the gunnery ranges below Cairnsmore of Fleet.

On occasion the crisis that spurred road building was more economic than military in nature. Following the failure of the 1846 potato crop in the Highlands, there was acute distress. Many faced starvation. To alleviate the intense poverty and suffering caused by famine, charitable relief was collected outside the

INTERIOR *of a* CROFTER'S HUT

Highlands and, together with contributions from landowners and county authorities, used to provide food for people in return for their work on road construction. The direct link between road making and the provision of famine relief led to these roads being known as 'Destitution Roads' – a name still applied to the road between Braemore Junction and DUNDONNELL in Ross & Cromarty.

The two mile length of road to Arnish on the ISLE OF RAASAY was built in response to frustration rather than destitution, but it is probably the most remarkable road in all

Scotland. Its construction dwarfs even the labour of Wade and Caulfeilds' soldiers – this road was built by one man with his own hands. This prodigious achievement was the backbreaking work of Calum MacLeod, who dug and pick-axed his way across rock and peat to link his house with the public road at Brochel. It took him more than ten years, eight shovels, six picks, four wheelbarrows and two hammers, plus gallons of sweat. Such a mammoth task was not embarked upon lightly. Indeed, it was undertaken only after repeated requests for a public road had gone unanswered. Such a road was needed to replace the path which provided the sole land link for the inhabitants of the area. Calum died in 1988 soon after completing his labour. His road, known as Calum's Road, has now been adopted and surfaced by the local authority and a cairn has been erected to his memory.

ROAD *to* DISASTER

Whilst Calum MacLeod's road was built as a lifeline, other builders have found themselves constructing a road to ruin. In 1817 the burgh of **ABERDEEN** was forced into bank-ruptcy by the construction of Union Street. This was an ambitious and overly expensive project since the road crosses a series of valleys and for about half a mile it is raised above the surrounding area on a succession of arches and bridges. Fortunately, the story had a happy ending as Trustees were appointed and the financial difficulties were resolved, leaving

Union Street not as a liability but as an asset to the city.

Whilst the cost of raising Union Street gave rise to problems, in most instances a raised section of road proved a blessing. The 'causey' was the raised central part of a street and was paved with stones or cobbles. Fine examples of original causeys can still be seen in an ancient burgh such as CULROSS, Dunfermline. Since the croun o' the causey (crown of the causeway) was the driest and least polluted section of a road, it was particularly popular with the wealthy on their perambulations. Naturally they expected others further down the social hierarchy to step aside into the muck-filled gutters when they passed.

The hazards facing those who ended up off the causey are illustrated by an entertaining eighteenth century account of a visit to IRVINE, Cunninghame, by Lord Eaglesham. He had come to visit land he had recently bought in the area. Just as his coach entered the narrow street – still called the Vennel – a line of coal-carts appeared at the other end. There was no room to turn and on trying to pass, his lordship's coach had to put its wheels off the causey and into the adjoining midden. This was when the fun for onlookers really started, for 'the horses gave a sudden loup, and couped the coach, and threw my lord head foremost into the very scent-bottle of the whole commodity, which made him go perfect mad, and he swore like a trooper that he would get an Act of Parliament to put down the nuisance'.

ROAD *to* ROMANCE

Poor road conditions, however, were not all bad news. The uneven, potted surface of the Old Luss Road in **HELENSBURGH**, Dumbarton, meant young ladies required assistance when walking along it. This proved 'an encouragement to fond declarations'. Consequently there was 'a fearful joy in the evening stroll which no smooth highway could ever impart … it was a highway to matrimony'.

The road to matrimony for many people in England led straight to Scotland. Following the 1754 Marriage Act, couples in England could not marry without parental consent before the age of 21 years. This compared with 16 years of age in Scotland, where all the couple had to do was to make a declaration before two witnesses. From 1856 it became necessary for one of the partners to have spent three weeks in Scotland before a marriage could legally take place. This relaxed system lasted until 1939 when the presence of a minister or registrar became necessary. Even today the minimum legal age for marriage remains lower in Scotland than in England – 16 compared with 18 years.

Runaway English couples made for the first building they came to across the Scottish border. Since this was often a tollhouse, it enabled tollkeepers to carry on a profitable sideline in marriage ceremonies. Runaway couples from England flocked to such tollhouses. The Sark Tollhouse at **GRETNA**, Annandale & Eskdale, which opened when the new turnpike road was built in 1830, proclaims itself as the first house in Scotland, and claims to have been the venue for 10,000 marriages. Until 1856, when the law changed, the attractive tollhouse at **COLDSTREAM**, Berwickshire, adjacent to the bridge across the border, was also the scene of numerous marriages.

Not everyone was so eager to rush into marriage. One of the saddest, most reluctant brides was a first century Pictish Princess, Deirdre NicCruithnigh – Deirdre of the Sorrows. At a young age she was betrothed by her father to the King of Ulster, Conchobar. She grew up in the area around Loch Etive, Argyll & Bute, in the company of the three sons of Uisneach. These idyllic days were brought to an end when Deirdre reached maturity and Conchobar's men came to escort her over to Ulster. Deirdre was loath to leave and only went on condition that the three brothers accompanied her. She took her leave of Scottish soil from the shores of Loch Etive.

The point of her departure is still marked by An Clach na Aiseag or 'The Farewell Stone' at Airds Bay near **TAYNUILT**, Argyll & Bute. Deirdre's anguish at leaving led her to compose and sing 'Farewell to Scotland'. Her heartfelt and moving song has survived the ages and is still sung. In Ulster she preferred the company of her three friends from home to that of Conchobar. The inevitable happened. The jealous king had the brothers killed and the distraught Deirdre died of a broken heart.

TRAVEL HAZARDS

Before the development of properly made
roads, travel was slow and often hazardous.
Finding the way could be a problem and in
the seventeenth century Archbishop Sharp
paid twelve Scotch shillings to 'a mane that
guydit the coatch'. As the Archbishop was to
discover to his cost, there were considerably
greater dangers than simply getting lost. On
3rd May 1679, the Archbishop's coach, in
which he was travelling with his daughter,
was waylaid by nine Covenanters and he
was mercilessly hacked to death before his
daughter's eyes. This gruesome scene is vivid-
ly portrayed on the Archbishop's monument
in Holy Trinity Church, St Andrews, North
East Fife. The motive for the attack was
Sharp's decision to switch his allegiance from
the Presbyterian to Episcopalian form of worship – no doubt for his own political reasons.

Highwaymen threatened travellers with
robbery as well as the possibility of murder.
A notorious local highwayman responsible, it
is thought, for a number of murders is buried
inside the unlikely setting of a church at
Balnakeil, Sutherland. His grave is built
into the south wall and inscribed:

> *Donald MakMurchou heir lyis lo*
> *Vas il to his freind var* [worse] *to his fo*
> *True to his maister in veird* [word] *and vo*
> [deed].

Donald was hardly the most popular of
people and he was concerned that his enemies

would seek vengeance by desecrating his grave. To prevent this, he is said to have paid Lord Reay £1000 to fund building work on the church provided that he could be buried within the building.

Inclement weather was another hazard facing travellers and a roadside memorial cairn near TWEEDSHAWS, north of Moffat, Tweed-dale, provides a reminder of this. Near this spot the driver and guard of the Edinburgh to Dumfries mail coach died in a fierce blizzard on 1st February 1831. The coach had become snowbound four miles to the south, but the two intrepid men had struggled on carrying the mailbags. They had unhitched two of the horses, but when the horses became tired they continued on foot until, overwhelmed by cold and exhaustion, they collapsed. Their snow-covered bodies were found four days later.

Whilst some have died trying to get the mail through, others have found themselves in trouble when the mail arrived. The citizens of HAWICK, Roxburgh, are still threatened with the dire warning on a Victorian letter box that 'letters which contain COIN if posted as ordinary letters will be charged on delivery with a special registration fee of eightpence'.

To help those out at sea, where the threat comes from bad weather, coastguards watched for ships in distress. At USAN, Angus, one of their watchtowers, although now a ruin, can still be seen. Apart from providing a viewing platform, it also housed life-saving apparatus. Such equipment, plus the heroism of a local girl, played an important part in a dramatic rescue near Aberdour Bay on the north coast of Banff & Buchan. In October 1844, 15 crew members of the steamer 'William Hope' were saved when Jane Whyte plunged into storm lashed seas to reach a life-line from the ship. A memorial to her is on the gable of her former cottage at ABERDOUR, Banff & Buchan.

On land, road travel became less of a risk in the eighteenth century following the creation of Turnpike Trusts. Their function was to raise money from tolls to build good quality roads between towns. Barriers were placed at intervals to prevent traffic using a road until a toll had been paid. The earliest barriers were often old pikeshafts – hence the name of 'turnpike'. Once the toll was paid the barrier was opened by the tollkeeper, who lived in the adjacent tollhouse.

Tolls varied according to the type of traffic, as shown by a rare example of an original tariff board which still exists on the tollhouse at Barnhill on the eastern outskirts of PERTH. Some financially astute travellers discovered ingenious ways of saving them-selves money. A carter with two horses could save 4d at the Barnhill Bar by unhitching one of them. It was cheaper for one horse to pull the cart (1s 0d) with the other going separately (0s 4d) than for the cart to be pul-led by two horses (1s 8d). The more audacious horse riders used to avoid paying tolls altogether by jumping the gates. Pedestrians were not charged, so one gypsy is reputed to have walked regularly through toll barriers carrying his donkey! Such methods of avoid-ing tolls will be hard for motorists to follow. In Fife there was a half-toll concession for 'a poor woman who earns a livelihood for herself and her aged, infirm husband by driving parcels and light goods from Cupar to the country around in a donkey cart'. One of the tollhouses participating in this scheme can still be seen in CUPAR, North East Fife.

To reduce the inconvenience to travellers, tollbars could not be less than six miles apart. The tollhouse at KINCAPLE, North East Fife, stretched this law to the limit in that it was very precisely positioned to ensure that the bar was placed fractionally beyond the six-mile stone on the Cupar to St Andrews road.

Tolls were never popular and resentment against paying sometimes spilled over into violence. In some places dismantling the local tollbar became a popular nocturnal activity and, on occasions, even the tollhouse was demolished. At DUNKELD, Perth & Kinross, the toll became even more unpopular following the arrival of the railway. The inhabitants of the town had to pass through the tollbar every time they went to the station at nearby Birnam. In 1868, anger finally boiled over into rioting. The tollgates were dumped in the River Tay, the tollhouse was attacked and general disorder broke out. This so frightened those in authority that troops were sent to restore order – a far cry from Dunkeld's tranquil image today.

The tollbars were closed at night to prevent the roads being used – a problem not faced by town dwellers. Nevertheless the poor quality of such street lighting as existed in burghs made travel in the dark unpleasant and sometimes dangerous. Those who could afford it either hired a horse-drawn hackney coach or were carried in a sedan chair. Sedan chairs were used in the eighteenth and early nineteenth centuries and had the big attraction that they could be brought right inside a house, providing not so much a door-to-door as a floor-to-floor service.

One of the more eccentric uses for a sedan chair was developed by an Edinburgh judge,

Lord Monboddo. While he chose to walk in the rain, his wig travelled separately in a sedan chair to keep it dry. To light the way for sedan chairs and the more affluent pedestrians, torches, ('links') were carried for a fee by link-boys. For economy, on completion of the trip the torches were extinguished in special link snuffers. A number of these can still be seen on the railings in front of the buildings on the north side of Charlotte Square, EDINBURGH.

LORD
MONBODDO
(*after* KAY)

For those travelling longer distances hackney coaches were used instead of sedan chairs. The fares, as with taxis today, were regulated. Examples of Post Chaise milestones are uncommon, but one can still be found in Woodhall Road, Colinton, EDINBURGH. This stone marks the five mile distance from the GPO in Edinburgh and was 'Erected to regulate the Post Horse duties payable by Hackney Coach 1824'.

The consequences of being run down by a sedan chair were unlikely to be too serious.

Since this was not the case with motor vehicles, they were viewed, at least initially, with great suspicion and to restrict their speed they had to be preceded by a person carrying a red flag. This could have led to the odd spectacle of a motor vehicle on an uncongested road being overtaken by a sedan chair. A notice on a bridge over the River Tay in Perth provides a reminder of those days. A by-law of 1878 required that:

> ... *no locomotive shall pass upon or over Perth Bridge between the hours of 10am and 3pm and that at other times the person in charge of such locomotive shall send a man with a red flag to the opposite end of the bridge from that on which he is to enter, warning all persons concerned of the approach of the locomotive before it shall go upon the bridge.*

Whilst the early motor vehicles did not exactly fly along, the same cannot be said of the adventurous Italian, Vincenzo Lunardi. On 5th October 1785 he ascended in a hydrogen balloon from the garden of Heriot's Hospital in Edinburgh and drifted across the Forth estuary to land east of CERES, North East Fife. The plaque marking his landing place claims this was the first aerial flight in Scotland. It fact this was not the case. Scotland's, and indeed Britain's, first manned aerial ascent was made the previous year in Edinburgh by a local man, James Tytler. On 27th August 1784 he ascended from near Holyrood to a height of about 350 feet and travelled half a mile, landing at Restalrig.

DIRECTIONS *and* MISDIRECTIONS

The difficulties of travelling by road were greatly reduced by the activities of the Turn-pike Trusts. Not only were road alignments and surfaces improved, but distances and directions started to be clearly shown on mile-stones and mileplates. Each Trust had its own distinctive 'house-style' of milestone, but no single one had a monopoly of curious features.

It is sometimes a mystery to the modern traveller why certain destinations are given prominence. A good example of this can be seen on the mileplate, dating from 1827, attached to the Mid-Steeple in DUMFRIES, Nithsdale. Amongst the places with distances shown to them is Huntingdon. It is not immediately apparent why anyone travelling through Dumfries should be interested in Huntingdon. It is, after all, difficult to imagine that the distance to Dumfries will be displayed prominently in the Huntingdon area. The answer to this puzzle lies in the soil, or at least in the grass. For those driving cattle rather than cars, Huntingdon once held considerable interest. In the early nineteenth century Dumfries was on the cattle drove route from Galloway to East Anglia where the animals were fattened on turnips for the London market. Huntingdon was a major market for selling the cattle, so the distance to it was important to the drovers of the past, if not to drivers of the present.

In Fife the frequent reference on milestones along the A92 to PETTYCUR near

Kinghorn, Kirkcaldy, is also a source of puzzlement to today's drivers – as it is not exactly a name that is on everyone's tongue. Until the coming of the railway, Pettycur, far from being a petty place, was an important ferry port. It was used regularly by traffic heading up the east coast from Edinburgh before the Forth Bridge was built.

Fife specialises in identifying unusual places that elsewhere are unlikely to be mentioned on milestones. In addition to the typical listings of towns and villages, milestones such as the one at the junction of the B9171 and B942 roads inland from ST MONANS, North East Fife, mention individual farms, mills and castles. A further feature is that directions show whether these buildings are off the road to the left or right.

Perhaps the most intriguing instance of a road with perplexing directions is the coastal stretch of the A719 where it turns inland south of DUNURE, Kyle & Carrick. Heading south the road appears to descend Croy Brae – or as it is better known, the Electric Brae. Any unsuspecting driver who slows down to admire the view and to let the car free-wheel down the hill is in for a shock, but not of the electric variety. Instead of the car continuing gently to descend, it appears to take on a mind of its own and start to ascend instead, thereby defying the laws of gravity. Sadly this seemingly magical power can be explained without resorting to supernatural forces. An optical illusion is at work, caused by the topography of the area. At this point the 'eyes' do not have it. Contrary to visual impressions the road actually ascends 13 feet between the west and east ends of this stretch of the hill.

Another unusual route that follows an unexpected direction is surely Scotland's strangest right of way – through the Inn at STRATHMIGLO, North East Fife. To record this fact, and to prevent any confusion, a sign above the passage door indicates the public right of way. It gives 24 hour access to Back Dykes but not to the bar!

Confusing directions are a problem facing unwary travellers along the A75 near CREETOWN, Wigtown. Responsibility for this situation lies not with the original road builders but with their modern successors, who clearly did not know if they were coming or going. When the road was widened in the 1980s, the commendable decision was taken to retain the old milestones, but unfortunately one of them has been replaced on the opposite side of the road. The arrow showing 3 miles to Newton Stewart in fact points *away* from the town and in the direction of Gatehouse of Fleet.

Some curious distances as well as directions are recorded in a few places. At least two milestones show the unexpected distance of '0' miles. The one at NEWPORT-ON-TAY, North East Fife, certainly leaves travellers who have crossed the Tay road bridge in no doubt as to where exactly they have ended up. In Strathyre, Stirling, a sign showing 'Inverlochlarig 8 and KINGSHOUSE 0' looks more like a shinty result than a mileplate.

Another unexpected distance is recorded on a milestone beside the A916 to the south of CUPAR, North East Fife. For reasons apparent to no one except the road surveyor concerned, some distances are shown in '1/7' miles. Since this is a multiple of neither rod, pole, nor furlong, the choice of this measure seems eccentric in the extreme. To further the mystery, other distances on this stone are shown in '1/3' miles as well as the more conventional units of '1/10'.

Although distances are shown it does not mean that they are necessarily accurate, as no doubt weary travellers have discovered to their cost. One of the milestones on the A823 shows a distance of '1/2' mile to RUMBLING BRIDGE, Perth & Kinross, and '6' miles to Dunfermline. Since it is ten and a half miles between these two places a quick calculation shows that something is amiss. Unfortunately when this marker was cast it seems that the figure '4' was inadvertently omitted.

Not only distances and directions are prone to error – spelling too can be faulty. At CARNWATH, Clydesdale, the town of Ayr is misspelt on the shaft of the market cross. It seems to have been the case that the mason was walking on Air instead of working on Ayr.

Sometimes the inclusion of a place name on a sign seems to be irrelevant to local people. This is well seen at CULROY, Kyle & Carrick, where there is an unexpected example of a road sign from the early days of motoring. It was erected by the Automobile Association and displays their logo. Apart from confirming that Culroy was – and still is – here, it continues to proclaim that it is only 5 miles to Ayr, but 398 to London. The second bit of information seems of less local use than the distance to Glasgow, which is not mentioned.

To anyone who has completely lost their sense of direction in the countryside, the sight of the familiar red telephone kiosk is likely to be welcomed. Whether the colour of the kiosk at **ACHFARY**, Sutherland is to be welcomed is perhaps debatable, but at least it is different and totally unexpected. For this kiosk has the distinction of being the only black and white one in Britain. The Achfary Estate was given special permission by the Post Office to blend the local kiosk in with the Estate's colour scheme.

The MURDER *of* ARCHBISHOP SHARP *in* 1679

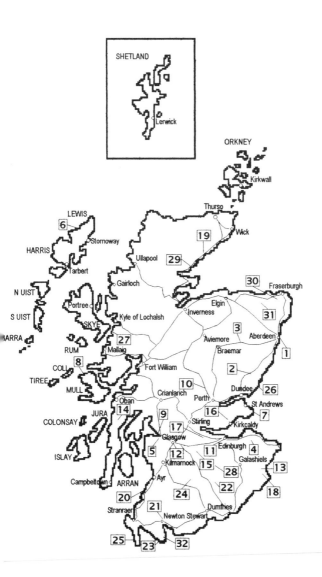

SHETLAND

Lerwick

ORKNEY

Kirkwall

Thurso

LEWIS
6
Stornoway

19

Wick

HARRIS

Ullapool
29

Tarbert

30 Fraserburgh

N UIST

Gairloch

S UIST

Portree

Elgin
Inverness

31

BARRA

SKYE

Kyle of Lochalsh

3
Aviemore

Aberdeen

RUM

27
Mallaig

Braemar

1

COLL
8

Fort William

2

TIREE

MULL

10
Crianlarich

Dundee
26

Perth

St Andrews

Oban

14

16

7

COLONSAY

JURA

9

Stirling

Kirkcaldy

17
Glasgow

5

12
Kilmarnock

11 Edinburgh
4

ISLAY

15

Galashiels

28

13

Campbeltown

ARRAN

Ayr

24

22

18

20
Stranraer

21

Dumfries

Newton Stewart

25

23

32

MAP 7 — CURIOUS CREATURES

CURIOUS CREATURES

Ref	Location	Description
1	Aberdeen	Kelly's Cats
2	Aberlemno	Pictish stone with battle scenes
3	Aboyne	Stones on Duchery Beg
4	Athelstaneford	Bull's head
5	Bishopton	Monkeys on roof
6	Bragar, Lewis	Whalebone arch and harpoon
7	Crail	Mercat cross and unicorn
8	Dervaig, Mull	Fish trap
9	Dumbarton	Geese on guard duty
10	Dunkeld	Buffalo Park
11	Edinburgh	Statue of Greyfriars Bobby
12	Glasgow	Ladybird on canopied chair
13	Kelso	Horseshoe
14	Kilmichael Glassary	Boar on rock
15	Lanark	Top dog
16	Leslie	Bull Stone
17	Linlithgow	Black Bitch
18	Linton	Worm/dragon in fight
19	Loth	Monument to killing of last wolf
20	Maidens	Spider – wall sculpture
21	Minnigaff	McClurg gravestone and ravens
22	Moffat	Ram statue
23	Monreith	Otter statue
24	Muirkirk	Gravestone called 'cat stone'
25	Port Logan	Fish pond
26	Saint Vigeans	Archer hunting stag
27	Sandaig	Memorial to otter
28	Skirling	Reptilian railings
29	Strath Carnach	World's oldest salmon ladder

CURIOUS CREATURES

A motley collection of birds, animals, fish, and even insects, with interesting or unusual stories associated with them, can be seen throughout Scotland. Animals include the wild, farm and domestic varieties.

FARM ANIMALS

It is not often that people look up to a sheep, especially in a town, but this happens in **MOFFAT**, Annandale & Eskdale, where an imposing ram on a pedestal looms over pedestrians in the main street. It has been doing this since the bronze statue was erected in 1875 as a tribute to the importance of sheep in the local economy – an interesting contrast in attitudes to the Highlands, where sheep are associated with the notorious Highland Clearances.

The other backbone of livestock farming is the cow. At first glance it is rather disconcerting to pass Athelstaneford Mains Farm near **ATHELSTANEFORD**, East Lothian, and see an impressive bull's head peering out from near the top of a large steading. Closer inspection shows that the head is not attached to a body and that it is simply an impressive decorative feature built of stone.

In contrast, a cow that proved very much

alive caused consternation in TURRIFF, Banff & Buchan. In 1913 Robert Paterson, who farmed locally at Lendrum, refused to pay the new National Insurance contributions of his employees. He was prosecuted and fined. When he refused to pay, one of his cows was poinded to be sold to pay the outstanding fine. The cow was to be auctioned off at Turriff market, but on market day the animal ensured immortality for itself by making its escape. What happened was that Paterson had painted 'LG & Coo Lendrum to Leeks' on the side of the animal as an insult to the government of the day led by Lloyd George, a Welshman. Turpentine was used to remove the paint and this maddened the cow, which broke free and ran amok through the centre of the town, causing pandemonium. Chaos ensued and Paterson, together with some of his associates, was arrested and charged with rioting. The case against them was found not proven. The cow was subsequently sent to market at Aberdeen, where it was bought by a group of farmers and presented back to Robert Paterson. This renowned 'Turra coo' is deservedly commemorated by a monument at the farm from where she was taken to be unwillingly sold.

The possibility of escaping must have been the dream of every bull subjected to the cruelties of bull-baiting. The animal was chained to a stake by the neck or leg and then set upon by a dog, which attempted to sink its teeth into the nose of the bull. It was not unknown for the bull to be further enraged by having pepper blown into its nostrils.

This vicious pastime was eventually banned in 1835, but its legacy is still in evidence at LESLIE, Kirkcaldy, in the shape of a Bull Stone on the village green. This granite rock, about three feet high, is deeply gouged with rope or chain marks made as the maddened beasts struggled to avoid their tormentors.

Cattle in Scotland may come in a range of shapes and sizes, but *buffalo*-shape is not one of them – usually. These creatures are normally associated with the dry plains of North America, not the damp hills of Scotland. Nevertheless buffalo, for a short time, roamed the Perthshire hills, a bizarre episode recalled in the name Buffalo Park near DUNKELD, Perth & Kinross. Buffalo, together with two Red Indians and a wild mountain man of mixed French and Cree Indian stock to look after them, were brought to the estate around Murthly Castle in 1839 by Sir William Stewart when he succeeded to the title of laird.

Sir William had visited North America and ended up fur trapping, mixing with Indians and mountain men, and hunting buffalo in the frontier lands of Wyoming. The house in which the Indians and mountain man lived are still there in the grounds of Murthly Castle, as is the building in which they sheltered when tending the animals on the hillside at Buffalo Park.

For a few years life was far from dull for the amazed local inhabitants. The climax came when Dunkeld was stirred from its slumbers one night by the memorable sight of the Indians and mountain man, roaring drunk, discharging pistols from a rowing boat, to

which they had attached wheels and which
was being pulled along the main street by a
pair of buffalo. Few residents complained
when, in 1842, Sir William decided to make
a return visit to North America. The Indians
and mountain man announced that they were
going too, never having adjusted to the
subtleties of the Scottish climate. The buffalo,
however, were made of sterner stuff – or just
possibly they were not asked. At any rate they
lived on in the area for a further 30 years.

DOMESTIC ANIMALS

In the past, horses rather than buffalo were the
usual means of transport and, like Cinderella,
they were prone to losing their shoes. The
horseshoe fixed into the road surface of
Roxburgh Street in KELSO, Roxburgh, is
associated not with a Prince Charming, but
with a Bonnie Prince – Charles Edward
Stewart. It is said to mark the spot where his
horse cast a shoe when his army passed
through the town at the time of the 1745
Rising. Both Charlie and, more especially, his
supporters, were to go on to lose much more
than a horseshoe following their defeat at
Culloden.

Horses seem to have been a great love of
the Picts – scenes including them are carved
with particular feeling and vitality on symbol
stones and cross slabs. The only symbol stone
with a large-scale and spectacular battle scene
involving horsemen is to be seen in the
churchyard at ABERLEMNO, Angus. This is
thought to portray the important battle of

DETAIL *of the* BATTLE SCENE *on the* ABERLEMNO STONE
(PHOTOGRAPH: PAUL TURNER)

Nechtansmere in AD 685, when the Picts
decisively defeated the invading Anglians
from Northumbria.

The opposing soldiers can be readily
distinguished. Those on the left-hand side
are bare-headed and appear to be the Picts,
whilst those on the right have helmets and
are thought to be the Anglians. The top row
shows a Pictish horseman pursuing one of the
invaders. The middle one portrays three
Pictish foot soldiers armed with shields and
spears fighting a mounted soldier.

The bottom row shows two rival horsemen coming to blows. The Anglian warrior
on his short-tailed horse is about to throw his
spear and he has used the bridle to steady
himself, thereby drawing back his horse's
head. The Pict, on his longer tailed horse,
has raised his shield to defend himself and is
preparing to counterattack with his spear. As
a result he has no hand on the reins: consequently his horse has its head held up high.

In the final scene the Anglian horseman lies dead and is about to be devoured as carrion by a large bird.

Pictish horses, no doubt, came in a wide range of colours, but a white horse is usually associated with a brand of whisky and found on bottle labels. However, near **STRICHEN**, Banff & Buchan, a giant white horse labels the side of Mormond Hill. It was cut into the quartzite rock in 1700 and is said to be the only one in Scotland. In England such horses are associated with Wessex rather than whisky.

The sight of three monkeys gamboling on a roof in Renfrew District is enough to make even the staunchest teetotallers wonder if they have been slipped some of the contents of the White Horse's bottle. Further investigation reveals yet more monkeys on neighbouring buildings, which are all part of the outbuildings for Formakin House near **BISHOPTON**, Renfrew. Not surprisingly this complex is known as the 'Monkey House'. Fully exposed to icy winds in winter, the monkeys could be expected to be of the brass variety, but instead they are frozen in stone. They are the work of the distinguished architect Robert Lorimer, who designed this group of buildings for the Paisley stockbroker and art enthusiast, John Homes, in the years prior to World War I. Holmes claimed the monkeys appealed to him because they were easily fed!

Another animal that has never been known to eat much, has the head and body of a white horse, the legs of a buck, the tail of a lion and a single horn. These are the distinctive features of a unicorn. This mythical beast is

much more common in Scotland than in
England, primarily because it was associated
with Scottish royalty. The old Royal Arms of
Scotland were supported by two unicorns and
can still be seen above the gatehouse to the
priory at WHITHORN, Wigtown.

The unicorn became a symbol of royal
patronage and is frequently portrayed on the
top of mercat crosses in the old royal burghs,
such as CRAIL, North East Fife. When James
VI of Scotland acceded to the British throne
in 1603, he insisted, not surprisingly, that
the Scottish unicorn should be incorporated
into the royal coat of arms. It supplanted the
red dragon of Wales and joined the English
lion as supporter of the Royal Arms – hence
the nursery rhyme 'The lion and the unicorn
were fighting for the crown'.

HUNTED ANIMALS

Royalty is often associated with the wild boar.
This is because boars were popular quarry to
hunt, and hunting rights, which were often
vested in the crown, were jealously guarded.
A boar was often used as a sign of kingship
and one can still be made out on a rock near

BOAR-HUNTING

the top of the small hill of Dunadd near KILMICHAEL GLASSARY, Argyll & Bute. The adjacent small basin and footprint, both carved out of the rock, were probably used in coronation ceremonies at Dunadd. At first sight this seems an unlikely place to find such royal insignia, but in the sixth century Dunadd became the capital of Dalriada. This was the kingdom first established by the Scots following their migration from Ireland.

A fine specimen of a boar, with sharp tusks, has been at the mercy of a hooded Pictish hunter since the early ninth century. This hunting scene, portrayed on the Drosten Stone at ST VIGEANS, Angus shows an archer in hooded camouflage about to fire an arrow from his bow. A little detective work reveals he is using the more powerful cross-bow rather than a long-bow. If it had been a long-bow, the archer would have been holding the bow itself, which is the part furthest away from him.

Stags are also a popular target for hunters. One such beast was killed by an exceptional piece of marksmanship in 1877. The shot was fired by William Cunliffe Brooks, an English millionaire and Member of Parliament. He had a passion for deer and in 1869 bought the Glentanar estate on Deeside to stalk and shoot them.

His efforts were crowned on 9th October 1877 by the remarkable feat of killing a parti-cularly elusive stag, nicknamed the 'Haunted Stag', at the almost unheard of distance of 267 yards. The sights on the rifle he used were generally considered to be inaccurate above about 170 yards. Brooks was so elated and proud of his marksmanship that he decided not to let posterity forget it. He built one stone marker, in the shape of a massive ball perched on a pyramid, at the spot where the stag fell – and another at the place he fired from, exactly 267 yards away. These monuments still stand on the hill of Duchery Beg, south of **ABOYNE**, Kincardine & Deeside. The inscription, now rather worn, includes his name, 'W Cunliffe Brooks MP'; the distance, '267 yards'; the target, 'The Haunted Stag'; the date, '9 October 1877'; and a verse:

The stag is dead
Availed not his swift power
Death's fangs
Sure bullet to its fatal mark has sped.

FAITHFUL FRIENDS

Some animals are remembered for being faithful rather than elusive, and none more so than dogs. In **LINLITHGOW**, West Lothian, a sign outside the Black Bitch Inn depicts a black greyhound which has become an emblem for the town. This faithful dog, or rather bitch, is reputed to have swum regularly across Linlithgow Loch, carrying food to its master, who had been tied to a tree on an island in the loch and left to starve to death. Who the dog's owner was, or why he was tied to a tree, have been lost in the mists of time, but the local people were sufficiently impressed by this event to adopt the black bitch and an oak tree as an alternative coat of arms to the one depicting St Michael. This makes Linlithgow very unusual in having two official coats of arms – all thanks to a dog.

The most impressive example of a dog's faithfulness to its master was displayed by Scotland's best-known dog – Greyfriars Bobby. This loyal Skye terrier is commemorated by an appealing statue at the top of Candlemaker Row in EDINBURGH. Recent evidence has revealed some inaccuracies in the popular version of the story, but the basic theme has been verified. Greyfriars Bobby's owner was John Gray, a policeman who lived near the Cowgate, in central Edinburgh. He was not, as usually portrayed, a shepherd in the Pentland Hills. Greyfriars Bobby was a policeman's watchdog and used to guard animal pens in the Grassmarket before the weekly market. He and his master probably did frequent the coffee-house in Greyfriars Place – now Greyfriars Bobby Bar – but it was not run then by John Traill, who subsequently claimed to have known Bobby and his master.

GREYFRIARS
BOBBY

John Gray died on 8th February 1858 and was buried in Greyfriars churchyard. His faithful dog, tradition claims, was reluctant to leave his master's grave and spent the next 14 years in or close to Greyfriars churchyard. He was fed and sometimes sheltered by kindly people who lived nearby and were touched by the dog's unwavering devotion to his master.

A genuine top dog can be seen in LANARK, Clydesdale, where it sits on top of the roof of a house in Castlegate. The stone figure of this

small canine is said to have been put up by a
Deacon MacDonald after his dog was poisoned.
He suspected that his neighbour – a Miss
Ingle – was responsible, and to make sure she
never forgot her callous deed he placed the
figure of his dog so that it looked down on
her whenever she left her house.

WILD ANIMALS

One member of the canine family that has had
a bad press, particularly in children's books,
is the much maligned wolf. Inevitably a wolf
would see domesticated animals as legitimate
food, but stories of attacks on people seem
suspect.

A fear of wolves, at times bordering on
paranoia, meant that people did not rest until
the last wolf was destroyed. At LOTH,
Sutherland, the slaying of the last wolf in the
district by a hunter called Polson, in about
1700, is commemorated by a monument.

Whilst a wolf's arch enemy has been man,
the traditional foe for a dog has been a cat.
The sight of a succession of cats along the
north parapet of the Union Street bridge in
ABERDEEN is sure to drive any self-respecting
dog to distraction. The cats have been in this
position for nearly 90 years and were used as
finials by Dr William Kelly when he designed
new parapets for the bridge. They were
supposed to be leopards, but have always
been known as 'Kelly's Cats'.

Although Aberdeen's unusual felines have
not attacked anyone, the same cannot be said
of other members of the cat family in

Scotland. In the churchyard at MUIRKIRK, Cumnock & Doon Valley, there is a gravestone showing the fierce head of a cat and two children. This commemorates two children who were killed by what was said to be a wildcat.

A particularly moving gravestone marks the last resting place of an animal, as well as the shattered dreams of an outstanding naturalist, at the lonely bay of SANDAIG, Lochaber, on the mainland opposite Skye. The animal was an otter and the naturalist was Gavin Maxwell. For 19 years Maxwell lived here at the place he called Camusfearna. In his classic book *Ring of Bright Water,* he wrote, 'wherever the changes of my life may lead me in the future, it will remain my spiritual home until I die'.

Maxwell lived simply, and close to nature, observing and writing about the wildlife around him, especially the otters. This period of his life was suddenly brought to a close in January 1968 by a disastrous fire, in which his house was destroyed and the otter, Edal, killed. Maxwell wrote: 'Tonight at the last sentence of a dream I stand in thought before the Camusfearna door. Someone, one day, perhaps, may build again upon that site, but there is much that cannot ever be rebuilt'.

The burial cairn of Edal states simply: 'Edal, The Otter of Ring of Bright Water, 1958-68 – whatever joy she gave to you give back to nature.'

Maxwell was brought up in Galloway and on rocks above the bay at **MONREITH**, Wigtown, near his family home, an otter is always visible. It is, in fact, a very life-like sculpture carved in memory of Edal.

CREEPY CRAWLIES

Just as Gavin Maxwell is always associated with otters, so Robert the Bruce is forever linked with spiders. It is doubtful if anywhere but Scotland can boast of a spider that changed the course of history. The famous encounter between the dispirited Bruce and a spider is portrayed on a wall decoration at the Bruce Hotel in **MAIDENS**, Kyle & Carrick. At the time Bruce was on the run from the English. Hiding in a cave, he watched a spider unsuccessfully but persistently try to spin a web. The spider's refusal to accept defeat paid off: the web was finally completed. Comparing his own situation to that of the spider, Bruce decided to battle on. Thereafter he never looked back. Bruce's campaign against the occupying English forces reached its climax with his victory at Bannockburn in 1314. This ensured Scotland's independence and his own title to the throne.

As any self-respecting entomologist knows, a spider is not an insect but an anachrid, whereas a ladybird is an insect through and through. Spiders may inhabit buildings as well as caves, but it is unusual, to say the least, to find a ladybird in permanent residence inside a cathedral. Nevertheless, **GLASGOW**'s Cathedral houses one. It sits on a canopied chair and is extremely life-like, although carved in wood. The chair, with its curious occupant, was gifted by the crew of a motor torpedo boat in gratitude for their survival after being sunk in action during World War II. It seems a ladybird had stowed away on their ship and was seen as a lucky omen.

BIRDS

Dark days of war are recalled by the curious sight of two ravens being pierced by a single arrow at MINNIGAFF, Wigtown. This scene is portrayed on a gravestone in the churchyard and is part of the coat of arms of the McClurg family. It recalls an event that took place nearby in 1307. In that year, during his campaign against the invading English forces, Robert Bruce stayed the night at Craigencallie, a cottage owned by the McClurg family near what is now Clatteringshaws Loch.

The three McClurg sons volunteered to join Bruce's forces, but first he insisted that they showed him their skills as archers. Three ravens were pointed out as suitable targets. The youngest son shot and missed, but the skills of his brothers saved the day. The second lad managed to shoot one of the ravens in flight and the other two birds, perched on a crag above the house, were killed by the third brother with a single arrow. Such skills were to contribute to Bruce's victory shortly afterwards at the Battle of Raploch Moss.

Robert the Bruce was a master of the surprise attack, but a valuable early warning system against such an eventuality can be

provided by birds, in the noisy shape of
geese. Such creatures proved their worth in
Roman times when they gave the alarm that
awoke the Roman garrison and alerted them
to the fact that the Gauls were scaling the
heights of the Capitol. Now, over 2000 years
later, geese are still employed in a similar role
in Scotland. A gaggle of geese are kept on
permanent guard duty to patrol the area
surrounding the Ballantyne's complex of
bonded whisky warehouses at DUMBARTON.
There are now about 100 geese and they have
been there since 1962.

SEA CREATURES *and* REPTILES

While ravens have been shot with arrows,
those giants of the oceans – whales – have
been hunted almost to extinction by means of
harpoons. The legacy of this slaughter
remains in arches made from the great jaws
of whales, which can be seen in a number of
places in Scotland. The most unusual of these
arches is to be seen at BRAGAR, Isle of Lewis.
In 1922 a blue whale was washed up on a
nearby beach. When it was examined it
became clear that, although it had been
harpooned, the detonator had failed to
explode. The whale must have escaped its
attackers, but the unfortunate creature then
went on to suffer a lingering and painful
death. The jawbones were erected to form an
arch and the harpoon head was hung from
them. A sad end to a noble creature.

Instead of risking life and limb on stormy
seas to catch fish, it is a lot easier if they can

be persuaded to come to the catchers. One way of facilitating this is to construct fish ladders by-passing natural obstacles such as waterfalls. Scotland has what is believed to be the world's oldest salmon ladder near the Torboll Falls in STRATH CARNACH, Sutherland. An alternative approach was adopted at PORT LOGAN, Wigtown, where an impressive tidal fish pond was blasted out of solid rock by Colonel Andrew McDouall of Logan. Completed in 1800, it is about 50 feet in diameter and 30 feet deep. The pond is linked to the sea by a narrow passage which can be blocked to allow the water in but not the fish out. The fish provided a very convenient supply of fresh meat for the estate. Over the years the pond has become home for tame and well-fed cod, which take food from the keeper's hand.

Another way of preventing fish from escaping is demonstrated by a salmon trap near DERVAIG, Isle of Mull. It consists of a low V-shaped drystone wall across the River Bellart where it enters the sea at Loch Cuin. At high tide the sea covers the trap, allowing the fish to enter the river. However, when the tide retreats, the water falls below the level of the stones, leaving the salmon trapped behind. The fish were shared out amongst the local people and the largest haul recorded was 60 salmon.

The local laird, who owned the fishing rights on the river, was less than enthusiastic. He consequently demanded that the trap should be removed. Since the locals knew a good thing when they saw one, they ignored his requests and took full advantage of the confused legal position over rights to the tidal portion of the estuary.

Such an unfriendly attitude towards the interests of local people would not have come from Lord Carmichael. This unpretentious and popular man had been governor, first of Victoria and then of Bengal, and in 1905 he built himself a fairly modest house in SKIRLING, Tweeddale. Lord Carmichael was passionately interested in art, being a trustee of both the National Gallery and the Scottish National Portrait Gallery, but throughout the village of Skirling he let his imagination and sense of humour run riot. He commissioned an entertaining collection of wrought-iron figures from Thomas Hadden, a prominent Edinburgh craftsman. Amongst the wrought-iron animals are some reptilian railings with strange lizard-like creatures clambering up them.

Reptiles such as dragons made a name for themselves by threatening local people in general and fair maids in particular, and then fighting gallant knights who came to rescue the intended victims. One such 'ravening beast' – looking like a cross between a giant worm and a dragon – is portrayed on a stone panel, carved in the twelfth century, above the door of the church at LINTON, Roxburgh. The creature is said to have terrorised the surrounding area and is shown fighting Sir John Somerville, the knight who killed it by putting a burning peat on the end of his lance and thrusting it down the beast's throat.

GEOGRAPHICAL INDEX

WESTERN & NORTHERN ISLES

Location	Map	Ref	Description	Directions
SHETLAND				
Eshaness	3	9	Gravestone of Donald Robertson killed in error	In graveyard
WESTERN ISLES				
Bragar (Lewis)	7	6	Whalebone arch and harpoon	In Bragar
Garry (Lewis)	5	15	Bridge built by Lord Leverhulme	At end of B895 above Garry Beach

NORTH HIGHLANDS

Location	Map	Ref	Description	Directions
INVERNESS				
Corrieyairack Pass	6	8	Wade road	Between upper reaches of River Spey and south end of Loch Ness

Location	Map	Ref	Description	Directions
Garvamore	6	22	Original King's House	At Garvamore on minor road W from Laggan
Invergarry	3	13	Well of the Heads	Near SW end of Loch Oich
ROSS & CROMARTY				
Cromarty	1	11	Tailor's sign	In Braehead
Dundonnell	6	16	Destitution Road	A832 between Dundonnell and Braemore Junction
Innis Maree	3	12	Oak tree with coins in it	On island in Loch Maree
Munlochy	3	23	Cloutie well	Beside A832 to W of village
Strathpeffer	3	32	Institution for Poor Spa Drinkers	Pump Room in the town
Tain	1	48	Tolbooth	In the High Street
SUTHERLAND				
Achfary	6	3	Black and white telephone kiosk	On A838 in village
Ardgay	1	2	White Stone	In village square
Balnakeil	6	4	Highwayman's gravestone	Inside ruined church NW of Durness
Bonar Bridge	5	9	Bridge with names of Parliamentary Commissioners	On A9
Dornoch	1	14	Ell	In churchyard of Cathedral

Location	Map	Ref	Description	Directions
Golspie	5	17	Parliamentary bridge	Across Golspie Burn
Helmsdale	5	20	Parliamentary bridge	Across River Helmsdale
Loth	7	19	Monument to killing of last wolf	Foot of Glen Loth on W side of A9
Rhiconich	3	28	Well for hospitality	7 miles NE of Rhiconich on A838
Strath Carnach	7	29	World's oldest salmon ladder	By-passes the Torboll Falls

WEST & CENTRAL HIGHLANDS

ARGYLL & BUTE

Location	Map	Ref	Description	Directions
Beinn Dorain	4	1	Mountain praised by Duncan Ban	5 miles N of Tyndrum
Dalmally	4	3	Duncan Ban MacIntyre's memorial	On hill at end of road SW of Dalmally
Dervaig (Mull)	7	8	Fish trap	Across mouth of River Bellart
Duntrune Castle	4	5	Ghostly piper	'Castle is on N shore of Crinan Loch
Glenbellart (Mull)	4	6	Bard writing of Clearances	Glenbellart – S of Dervaig
Isle of Colonsay	3	14	Lifting stone	On W side of island beside A870 above the golf course
Isle of Ulva	5	23	Tariff for dogs	List of old ferry tariffs in church

Location	Map	Ref	Description	Directions
Kilmichael Glassary	7	14	Boar on rock	On Dunadd Hill
Pennyghael (Mull)	3	26	Memorial to Beatons	Between A849 and the sea near Pennycross
River Lussa (Mull)	1	37	John Jones' grave	0.75 mile W of Ardura beside River Lussa
Taynuilt	6	38	The Farewell Stone	On shore by Airdsbay House
BADENOCH/STRATHSPEY				
Grantown-on-Spey	2	18	War-funded clock	On Speyside House in the town square
LOCHABER				
Sandaig	7	27	Memorial to otter	By beach about 5 miles SW of Glenelg
PERTH & KINROSS				
Aberfeldy	5	3	Wade's military bridge	Across River Tay
Auchterarder	2	3	Hour-glass	In church
Camusvrachan	3	6	Lifting stones	In field midway along Glen Lyon
Cashlie	3	7	Contraceptive stone	In field near road in upper Glen Lyon
Dunkeld	1	19	Ell	On Ell Shop in Market Square
Dunkeld	6	17	Tollhouse at centre of 1868 riots	S end of bridge across River Tay
Dunkeld	7	10	Buffalo Park	Near Rohallion House to SSE of Dunkeld

Location	Map	Ref	Description	Directions
Edendon Bridge	6	19	Wade's Stone	1.5 miles N of Edendon Bridge on E side of A9
Fearnan	3	10	Measles stone	In field by track to Boreland Farm above Loch Tay
Kenmore	5	24	Bridge funded by forced land sales	Across River Tay
Kinnoull	5	25	Ferryman on gravestone	In graveyard
PERTH & KINROSS				
Milton Eonan	3	20	Stone with Eonan's cross	E of Bridge of Balgie in Glen Lyon
Monzievaird	3	21	St Serf's Well	Beside the church on A85 between Crieff and Comrie
Muthill	2	22	Multiple dial	In gardens of Drummond Castle
Perth	3	27	Neo-classical water tower	E end of Marshall Place
Perth	6	31	Tollhouse with tariff board	At Barnhill 1 mile SE of town on A85
Perth	6	32	Notice on Perth Bridge re. red flag	On wall at E end of Perth Bridge
Rumbling Bridge	5	28	Double bridge	Where A823 crosses River Devon
Rumbling Bridge	6	34	Milestone with wrong distance	4th milestone S of Powmill on A823
Struan	3	33	Whooping cough stone	0.5 mile E of the church
Weem	6	41	General Wade's picture	On front wall of Weem Hotel

Location	Map	Ref	Description	Directions
SKYE & LOCHALSH				
Borreraig	4	2	Cairn on site of piping college	2 miles S of Dunvegan Head
Isle of Raasay	6	27	Calum's Road	Between Brochel and Arnish
Kilmuir	4	8	Gravestone of piper Charles MacKarter	Kilmuir graveyard
Snizort Church	1	39	Pedlar's murder	By A856 at Kensaleyre
NORTH EAST				
ABERDEEN				
Aberdeen	1	1	Mercat cross	E end of Union Street
Aberdeen	3	1	Inscribed water trough	Duthie Winter Garden
Aberdeen	3	2	Water tap with face	In Foordee
Aberdeen	5	1	Old Bridge of Dee	A92 across River Dee
Aberdeen	5	2	Brig o' Balgonie	Across R Dee 1 mile from where it enters the sea
Aberdeen	6	1	Road to bankruptcy	Union Street
Aberdeen	7	1	Kelly's Cats	On Union Street Bridge

Location	Map	Ref	Description	Directions
BANFF & BUCHAN				
Aberdour	6	2	Jane Whyte's memorial	Plaque on ruined mill on Aberdour Bay
Crimond	2	7	Clock with 61 minutes	On church
Fordyce	1	21	Minister threw snuff over wall	In churchyard
Longside	4	10	Jamie Fleeman's grave	In churchyard
Macduff	2	21	Faceless clock	On Doune Church
Strichen	7	30	White horse	On S side of Mormond Hill
Turriff	7	31	Memorial to Turra coo	At Lendrum Farm 4 miles SSE of Turriff
GORDON				
Kintore	1	25	Tolbooth	In village
KINCARDINE & DEESIDE				
Aboyne	3	3	Wells	On Wilcebe road – N side of Glentanar
Aboyne	7	3	Stones on Duchery Beg	Hill about 2 miles S of Aboyne
Drumlithie	2	9	Bell for weavers	Bell tower in village
Dunnottar	2	12	Hour-glass	In church
Fettercairn	1	20	Ell	On mercat cross in square

Location	Map	Ref	Description	Directions
Inverbervie	2	19	Tolbooth bell	In Church Street
Potarch	5	27	Bridge destroyed by floated timber	Across River Dee
Stonehaven	2	25	Pedestal sundial	By pier steps
Stonehaven	2	26	Barometer	In High Street
MORAY				
Burghead	3	5	Pictish well used for drownings	Seaward end of village
Dufftown	5	14	Disputed crossing	Across Dullan Water
Duffus	1	16	Mercat cross	In churchyard
Well of the Lecht	6	42	Stone plaque erected by 33rd Regiment	A939 1 mile N of Lecht summit

EAST & CENTRAL SCOTLAND

Location	Map	Ref	Description	Directions
ANGUS				
Aberlemno	7	2	Pictish stone with battle scenes	In churchyard
Glamis	2	17	Multiple dial	In grounds of Glamis Castle
Glamis	3	11	Pictish cross slab with cauldron/legs	In garden of manse

Location	Map	Ref	Description	Directions
Kirriemuir	1	27	Houses used as shops	By the churchyard
Logie Pert	5	26	North Water Bridge	Across N Esk River beside A94
Rescobie	1	36	Scooped-out measuring stone	Beside the church
St Vigeans	7	26	Archer hunting stag	Inside the museum in village street
Usan	6	40	Coastguard watchtower	In village street
DUNDEE				
Auchterhouse	1	3	Rush to pub after church	Church in village
DUNFERMLINE				
Culross	1	12	Sir George Bruce's house	W end of the Sandhaven
Culross	1	13	Flesher's sign	Near Mercat Cross
Culross	6	11	Croun o' the causey	In Wee Causeway and Stinking Wynd
Inchgarvie	5	21	Pillar of original Forth Rail Bridge	In River Forth with lighthouse on it
North Queensferry	3	24	Well with figures fighting	Lower part of The Brae
FALKIRK				
Airth	2	2	Sundial on mercat cross	In centre of Airth village
Glen Village	5	16	Faces on bridge	Across Union Canal

Location	Map	Ref	Description	Directions
KIRKCALDY				
Leslie	7	16	Bull Stone	On the green
Pettycur	6	33	Named on milestones	Milestones along A92
Windygates	2	29	Dairy clock	At crossroads in village centre
NORTH EAST FIFE				
Abdie	2	1	Sundial on Pictish stone	By church on S side of Lindores Loch
Anstruther Easter	5	5	Accident in Cunzie Burn	Cunzie Street
Anstruther Wester	5	6	Plaque – James V carried across Dreel burn	On Dreel Tavern
Ceres	1	7	Tron – carved on Weigh House	Now Fife Folk Museum
Ceres	1	8	Stone figure of Provost	On wall in the High Street
Ceres	6	6	Plaque to balloon trip	On dyke by B94 to S of North Callange
Crail	1	9	Custom House	In Shoregate
Crail	1	10	Wright's sign	Castle Street
Crail	2	6	Weather vane	On tolbooth
Crail	7	7	Mercat cross and unicorn	In Marketgate

Location	Map	Ref	Description	Directions
Cupar	6	13	Tollhouse	Junction of A91 and B940
Cupar	6	14	Milestone with 1/7 mile	On A916 4 miles S of Cupar
Dairsie	5	11	Bridge built by Archbishop Beaton	Across River Eden
Guardbridge	5	18	Bridge with arms of Arch. Beaton	Across River Eden
Kincaple	6	28	Tollhouse and bar at 6 mile mark	On A91 to N of Kincaple
Newport-on-Tay	6	30	Milestone with 0 miles	Centre of town
St Andrews	1	38	West Port	W end of South Street
St Andrews	6	35	Monument to Archbishop Sharp	In Holy Trinity Church
St Monans	6	36	Milestone with individual buildings	Junction of B942 and B9171
Strathmiglo	6	37	Right of way through inn	Strathmiglo Inn
Wormit	5	32	Old Tay rail bridge	Visible from B946
STIRLING				
Bannockburn	5	8	Bridge built due to a splash	Across the Bannock Burn
Callander	2	5	Sundial and verse	In South Church Street
Doune	1	15	Pistol making factory	Near centre of village
Doune	5	13	Bridge built to spite ferryman	Across River Teith

Location	Map	Ref	Description	Directions
Dunblane	2	11	Weather vane	On top of Cathedral
Killin	3	15	St Fillan's healing stones	Kept in Tourist Information Centre
Kilmadock	1	24	Pistol makers	Old graveyard 1 mile to W of Doune
Kingshouse	6	29	Milestone with 0 miles	Opposite Kingshouse Hotel in Strathyre
Stirling	1	43	John Cowane's statue	On the Guildhall – formerly Cowane's Hospital
Stirling	1	44	Old Brig	Across River Forth on N side of town
Stirling	1	45	Guildhall	Beside Holy Rood Church
Stirling	1	46	Robert Spittal's House	Spital Street
Stirling	1	47	Merchants' reversed 4 sign	On lamps outside the Guildhall

WEST OF SCOTLAND

CLYDESDALE

Location	Map	Ref	Description	Directions
Carnwath	6	5	Ayr mis-spelt	On mercat cross in main street
Douglas	2	8	Clock chimes early	St Brides Church
Lanark	7	15	Top dog	On roof of 15 Castlegate

Location	Map	Ref	Description	Directions
New Lanark	1	31	Philanthropic development	Village of New Lanark
New Lanark	2	23	Bell brought by Highlanders	On top of New Buildings
CUNNINGHAME				
Irvine	6	26	Coach crash	In the Vennel in centre of town
DUMBARTON				
Dumbarton	7	9	Geese on guard duty	At Ballantine's whisky warehouse complex
Helensburgh	6	25	Highway to matrimony	Old Luss road
GLASGOW				
Glasgow	1	22	Templeton's carpet factory	By Glasgow Green
Glasgow	7	12	Ladybird on canopied chair	Inside Glasgow Cathedral
HAMILTON				
Hamilton	5	19	Bridge built due to missed meeting	SE of town across River Avon
INVERCLYDE				
Port Glasgow	1	34	Stakes in mud	E side of town in River Clyde
KILMARNOCK & LOUDOUN				
Stewarton	1	42	Inscription 'No mill no meal'	On gable of Millhouse Hotel in High Street

Location	Map	Ref	Description	Directions
RENFREW				
Bishopton	2	4	Text about time	Formakin House
Bishopton	7	5	Monkeys on roof	Formakin House
Kilbarchan	4	7	Habbie Simpson's statue	On tower in village centre
Kilmacolm	3	16	St Fillan's Well	2 miles to SE on road to Houston

SOUTH EAST SCOTLAND

Location	Map	Ref	Description	Directions
BERWICKSHIRE				
Bunkle	1	6	Pedlar's gravestone	In old churchyard about 3 miles W of Auchencrow
Coldstream	6	7	Toll House	N end of bridge across River Tweed
Eyemouth	2	16	Memorial to storm victims	In old graveyard near seafront
Westruther	2	28	Coaching clocks	3 miles SW of Westruther on A697
EAST LOTHIAN				
Athelstaneford	7	4	Bull's head	Athelstaneford Mains Farm
Bolton	3	4	Well inscribed to Burns' mother	1.5 miles SW of Haddington by A6137

Location	Map	Ref	Description	Directions
Dunbar	1	18	Tolbooth	In High Street
Dunbar	2	10	Barometer pedestal	By harbour
Haddington	1	23	Stent Stane	Junction of High Street and Hardgate
Musselburgh	1	29	Tolbooth	In High Street
Ormiston	1	32	Mercat cross	In centre of village
Preston	1	35	Mercat cross	Just N of A198 close to link road into village
Stenton	1	41	Tron	In centre of village
Stenton	3	31	Mediaeval well	NE end of village
Wester Pencaitland	2	27	Sundial on mercat cross	In village
EDINBURGH				
Edinburgh	2	13	Clock on Balmoral Hotel	Princes Street
Edinburgh	2	14	Hour-glass	Corstorphine Old Parish Church
Edinburgh	6	20	Link snuffer	N side of Charlotte Square
Edinburgh	6	21	Post Chaise milestone	In wall opposite 39 Woodhall Road, Colinton
Edinburgh	7	11	Statue of Greyfriars Bobby	Candlemakers Row
South Queensferry	2	24	Mass dial	S wall of St Mary's Church

Location	Map	Ref	Description	Directions
South Queensferry	5	30	Forth Rail Bridge	Spans River Forth
ETTRICK & LAUDERDALE				
Stow	5	31	Collection bridge	Across Gala Water
ROXBURGH				
Hawick	6	24	Warning on Victorian letter box	Wall of Sandbed Post Office
Kelso	7	13	Horseshoe	In the road in Roxburgh Street
Linton	7	18	Worm/dragon in fight	Above entrance to the church
TWEEDDALE				
Dewar's Gill	4	4	Piper's grave	At highest point of B709 N of Innerleithen
Innerleithen	5	22	Vacant stipend bridge	N side of village across Leithen Water
Peebles	1	33	White Stone	On A72 opposite entrance to Peebles Hydro
Skirling	4	11	Sad piper	On building overlooking village green
Skirling	7	28	Reptilian railings	Outside Skirling House by village green
Tweedshaws	6	39	Memorial cairn to mail coachmen	Beside A701, 7 miles N of Moffat
WEST LOTHIAN				
Bo'ness	1	4	Sea Box Society crest	On building in Corbiehall

Location	Map	Ref	Description	Directions
Bo'ness	1	5	Reversed 4/sailing ship on gravestone	Bo'ness Old Kirk graveyard
Linlithgow	1	28	Cordiner's sign	On building at 123 High Street
Linlithgow	2	20	'Wee Meg Duncan' bell clapper	In tower of St Michael's Church
Linlithgow	3	19	Carved wellhead – St Michael's Well	High Street
Linlithgow	4	9	Carved drummers	The Cross Well
Linlithgow	7	17	Black Bitch	Sign on pub at the West Port

SOUTH WEST SCOTLAND

ANNANDALE & ESKDALE

Location	Map	Ref	Description	Directions
Ewes	2	15	Bell up tree	In churchyard
Gretna	6	23	Sark Toll House	First building on Scottish side of Border
Moffat	7	22	Ram statue	In main street

CUMNOCK & DOON VALLEY

Location	Map	Ref	Description	Directions
Muirkirk	7	24	Gravestone known as 'cat stone'	In churchyard
Stair	1	40	Tam o' Shanter and Water of Ayr Hone Co.	Upstream from bridge over River Ayr

Location	Map	Ref	Description	Directions
KYLE & CARRICK				
Alloway	5	4	Tam o' Shanter and witches	Auld Brig o' Doon
Ayr	5	7	Auld Brig's debate with New Brig	Across River Ayr
Culroy	6	12	Old AA plaque	In village on B7024
Dunure	6	18	Electric Brae	1 mile S of Dunure on A719
Maidens	7	20	Spider – wall sculpture	At Bruce Hotel
Old Dailly	3	25	Lifting stones	In churchyard of ruined church
NITHSDALE				
Dumfries	1	17	Ell	On Mid Steeple in the High Street
Dumfries	6	15	Mid Steeple mileplate	In the High Street
New Abbey	1	30	Blacksmith's sign	On building in main street
Ruthwell	3	29	Brow Well	1 mile SW of Ruthwell on B725
Sanquhar	5	29	Glenairlie Bridge	4.5 miles SE of Sanquhar across River Nith
STEWARTRY				
Dalbeattie	3	8	Slot Well	On S side of Buittle Hill to W of Dalbeattie
Dalry	5	12	Bridge built by local tailor	2 miles NW of Dalry over Polharrow River

Location	Map	Ref	Description	Directions
Kirkcudbright	1	26	Billy Marshall's gravestone	In graveyard beside A727
Kirkcudbright	3	17	Well and inscription	By tolbooth
Kirkpatrick Durham	3	18	St Patrick's Well	1 mile to NE of Kirkpatrick Durham
WIGTOWN				
Creetown	5	10	Beardie's Bridge	Across Balloch Burn in village
Creetown	6	9	Tank Road	0.75 mile N of Creetown by old railway
Creetown	6	10	Milestone pointing wrong way	3 miles SE of Newton Stewart on A75
Minnigaff	7	21	McClurg gravestone and ravens	In the churchyard
Monreith	7	23	Otter statue	Beside road above Kirkmaiden Churchyard
Mull of Logan	3	22	Dropping Cave	On coast just N of Mull of Logan
Port Logan	7	25	Fish pond	N side of Port Logan Bay
Sorbie	3	30	Source of leeches – White Loch of Ravenstone	2.5 miles SW of Sorbie
Whithorn	7	32	Unicorns	On Whithorn Priory gatehouse

*Denotes that the Curiosity is on private property or kept locked

133